PRAISE FOR *THE RIGHT*

"Popular wisdom says we need more self-love, self-affirmation, self-assurance to become confident women. But Mary Kassian counters this well-worn self-help solution. *The Right Kind of Confident* is thought-provoking. Eye-opening. Inspiring. It takes us on a journey to discover that the fear of the Lord is the key to overcoming our personal fears and insecurities. Young or old, you need the wisdom found in these pages! When you embrace God's confidence formula, you'll become a super-confident woman who can face even the most daunting circumstance with remarkable strength and courage."

—NANCY DEMOSS WOLGEMUTH, AUTHOR OF *LIES WOMEN BELIEVE* AND *ADORNED*, FOUNDER OF REVIVE OUR HEARTS, AND BIBLE TEACHER

"Mary brings the WORD. She's counterculture in all the best ways. She breaks down the popular self-help lies and shows us a more Christ-centered way to true confidence. If you're sick of living in fear and being a slave to everyone else's opinions about who you should be, this book is for you. Great work, Mary! What a timely message."

—KRISTEN CLARK AND BETHANY BEAL, AUTHORS OF *GIRL DEFINED* AND FOUNDERS OF GIRL DEFINED MINISTRIES

"I grabbed a pen as I read Mary Kassian's *The Right Kind of Confident*, and I underlined this: 'Do you want to be a confident woman? One who possesses great calmness, great boldness, and the ability to face trouble with the most mighty and invincible spirit in the world?' I scrawled, 'Yes!' in the margin and dug in deeper. I wasn't disappointed. This book is packed with 'here's why' and 'how to' for women who want to move forward in faith and not give way to fear. Mary Kassian doesn't shy away from tough questions and honest answers. She helps us to discover why we want confidence (and God's good purpose for it), what we misunderstand about fear (and God's good purposes for *it*), and how the whole trajectory of our lives is skillfully shaped by our heavenly Father who doesn't have a doubt in the world about his love or plan for us."

—LAURA BOOZ, AUTHOR AND PODCAST HOST OF *EXPECT SOMETHING BEAUTIFUL*

"With the heart of a teacher and the compassion of a friend, Mary shows us from Scripture what it means to be truly confident women who fear the Lord and place our trust in him. I appreciate her perceptive diagnosis of what's gone wrong within our hearts and the clarity with which she leads us to the only solution: a greater awe and worship of Jesus Christ and obedience and devotion to him who alone is to be feared. This is the right kind of confidence indeed!"

—KRISTEN WETHERELL, AUTHOR OF *FIGHT YOUR FEARS*

"*The Right Kind of Confident* is a message I want every woman to hear! While the world holds up self-worth and self-esteem as the way to be fearless and confident, Mary Kassian encourages women to rightly orient their fear toward the only One who is worthy of it. This book will help you joyfully endure even the most challenging circumstances with a well-placed confidence in the Lord."

—HUNTER BELESS, FOUNDER OF JOURNEYWOMEN AND
HOST OF THE *JOURNEYWOMEN* PODCAST

"'Self-confidence is the antidote!' the world says in response to your anxiety spikes and crippling self-doubt. But what if your fear-fed insecurity is being manufactured by a slithering con artist? What if it's your *enemy* suggesting your confidence should be in you? With her trademark clarity and biblical wisdom, Mary brilliantly pulls back deceit's curtain and reveals how fragile and self-destructive our self-confidence truly is, then she trains us to see our fears as God's invitations to draw near and sink our roots more deeply into him. Come learn to fear everything else less by fearing God more—which is the way to grow the *right* kind of confidence."

—SHANNON POPKIN, AUTHOR OF *CONTROL GIRL* AND *COMPARISON GIRL*

"Let's be honest, girls; we've got a confidence problem. The world's constant efforts to pump us up with messages of our 'enoughness' don't work. We know we're weak. We *know* we don't have what it takes to face life as broken women in a broken world. We know that confidence in ourselves falls flat every single time. I am so grateful for Mary Kassian's book *The Right Kind of Confident.* This is the countercultural message we've been looking for! The world's definition of confidence is dead wrong. Mary's book is a beautiful reminder that the right kind of confidence flows from our confidence in Christ."

—ERIN DAVIS, AUTHOR AND PODCASTER SEEKING
TO FIND HER CONFIDENCE IN CHRIST

THE RIGHT KIND OF CONFIDENT

THE RIGHT KIND OF CONFIDENT

THE REMARKABLE GRIT OF
A GOD-FEARING WOMAN

MARY A. KASSIAN

NELSON
BOOKS

An Imprint of Thomas Nelson

Published in Nashville, Tennessee, by Nelson Books, an imprint of Thomas Nelson. Nelson Books and Thomas Nelson are registered trademarks of HarperCollins Christian Publishing, Inc.

Published in association with the literary agency of Wolgemuth & Associates, Inc.

Thomas Nelson titles may be purchased in bulk for educational, business, fundraising, or sales promotional use. For information, please e-mail SpecialMarkets@ThomasNelson.com.

Unless otherwise noted, Scripture quotations are taken from the ESV® Bible (The Holy Bible, English Standard Version®). Copyright © 2001 by Crossway, a publishing ministry of Good News Publishers. Used by permission. All rights reserved. Scripture quotations marked CSB are taken from the Christian Standard Bible®. Copyright © 2017 by Holman Bible Publishers. Used by permission. Christian Standard Bible® and CSB® are federally registered trademarks of Holman Bible Publishers. Scripture quotations marked KJV are taken from the King James Version. Public domain. Scripture quotations marked NIV are taken from the Holy Bible, New International Version®, NIV®. Copyright © 1973, 1978, 1984, 2011 by Biblica, Inc.® Used by permission of Zondervan. All rights reserved worldwide. www.zondervan.com. The "NIV" and "New International Version" are trademarks registered in the United States Patent and Trademark Office by Biblica, Inc.®

Any internet addresses, phone numbers, or company or product information printed in this book are offered as a resource and are not intended in any way to be or to imply an endorsement by Thomas Nelson, nor does Thomas Nelson vouch for the existence, content, or services of these sites, phone numbers, companies, or products beyond the life of this book.

ISBN 978-1-4002-0987-3 (eBook)
ISBN 978-1-4002-0986-6 (TP)

Library of Congress Cataloging-in-Publication Data

Names: Kassian, Mary A. author.
Title: The right kind of confident : the remarkable grit of a God-fearing woman / Mary A Kassian.
Description: Nashville, Tennessee : Nelson Books, [2021] | Includes bibliographical references. | Summary: "Mary Kassian shows readers how they can be transformed into bold, indomitable women when they develop a reverent fear of God that rejects the wrong and embraces the right kind of confidence"-- Provided by publisher.
Identifiers: LCCN 2021011138 (print) | LCCN 2021011139 (ebook) | ISBN 9781400209866 (paperback) | ISBN 9781400209873 (epub)
Subjects: LCSH: Christian women--Religious life. | Self-confidence--Religious aspects--Christianity.
Classification: LCC BV4527 .K374 2021 (print) | LCC BV4527 (ebook) | DDC 248.8/43--dc23
LC record available at https://lccn.loc.gov/2021011138
LC ebook record available at https://lccn.loc.gov/2021011139

Printed in the United States of America
21 22 23 24 25 LSC 10 9 8 7 6 5 4 3 2 1

For Nanette, Michele, and Aileen

confidence

[**kon**-fi-d*ə*n*s*]

noun

1. trust or faith in a person or thing
2. belief in yourself and your abilities
3. certitude; assurance

In the
FEAR OF THE LORD
one has
STRONG CONFIDENCE.

Proverbs 14:26

CONTENTS

PREFACE

Today's woman has a confidence problem. All her life she has been raised to be a strong, confident woman. Yet deep inside, she harbors an embarrassing secret. She lacks a firm faith in her own abilities. She feels weak. She's not nearly as strong and confident as she makes herself out to be. Her confidence is fleeting. Often, it's phony—a well-crafted performance intended to suppress underlying currents of self-doubt.

She frequently fears she does not have what it takes. The fretting, second-guessing, and negative self-talk swirl around her mind like tumbleweeds down the dusty street of an old spaghetti western. Reruns of the same old movie keep her awake at night. She can't seem to shake the feeling that she is not good enough, that no matter how hard she tries, she's doomed to fail.

What can we do about this lack of confidence?

How do we transform our *can't-do* into a *can-do*?

How do we turn our cowardice into bravery?

How can we silence the nagging fears that sabotage and cripple us?

Popular authors say the answer is to believe in ourselves more and work to develop more self-confidence. Greater self-assurance will defeat the fear that stands in the way of our success.

But haven't we already tried the self-affirmation solution? Will more rah-rah girl power genuinely quiet the insecurity and self-doubt gnawing at our souls? Could it be that there is something missing in this well-worn confidence formula?

The Bible provides a different solution.

A counterintuitive solution.

It teaches that the way to combat fear is with more fear—fear of a different kind.

Most of us think that *all* fear is *bad* fear. But the Bible reveals that this is not the case. Fear also has a largely neglected positive dimension. The negative and positive types of fear are like opposite sides of a coin. And, paradoxically, Scripture suggests that a negative fear can only be overturned by embracing a positive one.

Proverbs 14:26 makes this clear. It informs us that "in the fear of the LORD one has strong confidence."

Fear and confidence. They go together like lightning and thunder, salt and pepper, Jack and Jill. To be confident women, therefore, we need to understand a whole lot more about the positive type of fear that the Bible identifies as confidence's close companion.

In this book, we'll do just that.

We'll start, in chapter 1, by figuring out the meaning of confidence and examining what the Bible upholds as the right formula for confidence. In chapters 2 to 4, we'll explore the topic of fear, including how fear works, how it runs amok, and the negative and positive aspects of this powerful emotion. In the final three chapters, we'll turn our attention to how the right kind of fear helps us build the right kind of confidence.

Seven chapters in all.

I suggest that you read and study this book together with a group of friends. It's chock-full of biblical instruction on how to grow confidence. To that end, I've compiled chapter questions and exercises to help you apply the material. You can download the chapter questions and a leader guide on my website, www.MaryKassian.com or www.RightKindOfConfident.com.

You'll benefit from completing the chapter questions even if you work through the book alone. Make sure to download the files ahead of time so you can reflect on the questions as you read. Tuck them into the back of your book for easy reference or perhaps into your journal to use as journaling prompts.

The fact that you're reading this preface tells me that the prospect of growing more confident piques your interest. Maybe you feel fearful and want to learn how to overcome personal insecurities. Maybe you generally feel confident but are facing an especially difficult challenge that is shaking you. Maybe you are looking for an overall confidence boost. Or perhaps you generally feel confident, but as a Christian, you want to make sure it's the right kind of confident.

Regardless of the reason you picked up this book, I think that reading it will help. At the very least, it should challenge you to rethink what you believe about this important topic.

But in the end, I hope it will do a whole lot more than that. I pray that the Lord will use these pages as a catalyst

- to help you put fear in its place and open your eyes to the power and beauty of our mysterious, fearful, and fascinating Lord;
- to bring you to a jaw-dropping, knee-knocking, pulse-quickening awareness of God's glory that shakes you to the core and radically reorients your perspective; and
- to help you break free from all the fears that have tripped you up and kept you down for as long as you can remember.

As you put fear in its place, you will grow bolder, braver, and more certain. You'll become a gutsy woman with remarkable grit.

Daring.

Determined.

Undaunted.

Reverent fear will help defeat your fear of other things—so that even your deepest fears can be met with a mirror response of courage.

You will become a strong, confident woman—the *right* kind of confident.

1

A BLUEPRINT FOR CONFIDENCE

What we need is a blueprint for confidence,
a confidence code, if you will, that will get
women headed in the right direction.

–Katty Kay and Claire Shipman, *The Confidence Code*

Women have a glaring problem. A problem we rarely talk about.

Though we have gained competence, we still lack confidence. Though we can freely chase our dreams, we still trip over our insecurities. Though we've been groomed to brim with self-assurance, we are still mired in self-doubt.

The all-important question that Sheryl Sandberg, the chief operating officer of Facebook, has challenged women to consider is this: "What would you do if you weren't afraid?"[1]

Sandberg's foray into the public eye began at the 2010 TEDWomen conference.

Power-dressed in a simple gray tunic, classic black pencil skirt, and high-heeled pumps, she stood poised in the middle of the large red speaker's circle, the mainstay of TED Talks.

Immense statues flanked the stage, keeping watch over her oration like the Greek Colossus of Rhodes guarding the Mandraki harbor. A towering, fifty-foot-high LED screen exponentially magnified Sandberg's image, giving her a larger-than-life presence. It was a wildly impressive set—even by TED standards.

Sandberg's audience listened with rapt attention as she calmly explained why women aren't making it to the top. Part of the problem, she argued, is the attitude of men. But another part is the fearful mindset of women. Women have internal obstacles standing in the way of their success. And one of the greatest obstacles is a lack of self-confidence.[2]

"We hold ourselves back in ways both big and small, by lacking self-confidence, by not raising our hands, and by pulling back when we should be leaning in," she later wrote in her *New York Times* bestselling book.[3]

Fear is the biggest culprit. Without fear standing in the way, women would be free to pursue both professional success and personal fulfillment. "Fear is at the root of so many of the barriers that women face. Fear of not being liked. Fear of making the wrong choice. Fear of drawing negative attention. Fear of overreaching. Fear of being judged. Fear of failure."[4]

What would you do if you weren't afraid?

It's a good question. One that, for most of us, touches a nerve. Because if we're honest, we must admit that fear *does* hold us back. There are many things we would do if only we weren't afraid.

Sandberg's original talk lasted less than fifteen minutes. But like a stone interrupting the still surface of a pond, it had a profound ripple effect. The video of her talk went viral, attracting millions of views. Her ensuing book, *Lean In*, quickly became a cultural phenomenon.

Sandberg packed theaters, dominated opinion pages, was featured on the covers of magazines like *Time* and *Fortune*, and appeared on every major TV talk show, including *60 Minutes* and *Nightline*.[5] She founded a global nonprofit organization called Lean In to help women face their fears and achieve their ambitions.

And that's not to mention the spin-off books and products, interviews, articles, tightly integrated Facebook community, and tens of thousands of Lean In Circles in 184 countries that came into existence.[6] Untold numbers of women were swept up in the wake of the excitement.

Why? What is the appeal? Why are women so hungry for Sandberg's message to lean in?

On the surface, the enormous response is puzzling.

The idea that a woman should believe in herself has been promoted for decades. It was 1972 when Helen Reddy's iconic pop song "I Am Woman (Hear Me Roar)" hit the top of the charts. Since that time, a steady stream of girl bands and girl-power anthems have reinforced the message that women are strong and invincible simply by virtue of being female.

Girls' T-shirts blaze with common slogans like:

Girl Power!
Hear Me Roar!
Girls Can't What?!
Out of the Kitchen and Into the White House!
The Future Is Female!

I Am My Own Superhero!
Who Runs the World? Girls!
We Can Do It!

For more than half a century, self-affirmation messages have run on auto repeat like the only song on the modern woman's playlist. Pop culture has served up a feminist smorgasbord for decades. Sandberg's entrée uses the same ingredients. So why are women so ravenous for her dish? What's the star ingredient in her recipe? Which flavor has she accentuated that creates such an enticing aroma?

Simply this: *confidence.*

Sandberg exposed a painful truth that women rarely talk about.

We are not living up to what we are expected to be.

Culture has raised us to be strong, confident women. Yet though we appear confident on the outside, on the inside we are not.

To borrow the analogy of Arianna Huffington, founder of the *Huffington Post*, it is as though a woman has an obnoxious roommate living in her head, telling her that her idea won't work, that the question she wants to ask is dumb, that she should not try because she will inevitably fail, and that she should inconspicuously hang out in the corner because, on top of everything else, she's having a really bad hair day.[7]

In the *New York Times* bestseller *The Confidence Code*, journalists Katty Kay and Claire Shipman mimic Sandberg's claim that self-confidence is the key to women's personal and professional success. They also echo her concern that, in women, confidence is in alarmingly short supply.

Self-doubt is a "dark spot" that plagues even the most accomplished of us.

As we talked to women, dozens of them, all accomplished and credentialed, we kept bumping up against a dark spot that we couldn't quite identify, a force clearly holding us back. . . . In two decades of covering American politics, we have interviewed some of the most influential women in the nation. In our jobs and our lives, we walk among people who you'd assume would brim with confidence. On closer inspection, however, with our new focus, we were surprised to realize the full extent to which the power centers of this nation are zones of female self-doubt.[8]

The powerful women that Kay and Shipman interviewed were "fantastically capable."[9] Yet oddly, they still lacked confidence. For some of these high achievers, the very subject was uncomfortable; it revealed a weakness they were reluctant to admit they had.

Women have a self-confidence problem.

They lack the confidence that men seem to have in droves.

This lack of confidence, though, isn't confined to women who walk the corridors of power in Washington or occupy corner offices in corporate America. Indeed, if *those* women struggle, just imagine what it's like for the rest of us.

You've undoubtedly sensed those disquieting emotions gnawing at the pit of your stomach: The hesitancy to speak up for fear that you'll embarrass yourself or say something stupid. The reluctance to volunteer for a position because you're afraid you'll disappoint. The agonizing distress that someone will poke a hole through your fragile veneer and discover that you are an impostor.

These feelings are inside us all. We just keep them stuffed down where no one can see.

Whether you are

- white-collar or blue, boardroom or mudroom, skyscraper or barn;
- spikes or sandals, designer or thrift, petite or plus;
- pop or hip-hop, salad or steak, Prius or Ram . . .

Whether you spend your day changing dirty diapers or negotiating corporate deals, chances are you also struggle with insecurities, fears, and self-doubt.

Wouldn't it be nice to find a way to conquer all those nagging negative thoughts and feelings?

THE STAKES ARE HIGH

Numerous academic studies confirm that fear is crippling women.

The "2016 Dove Global Beauty and Confidence Report," based off interviews with 10,500 females across thirteen countries, found that insecurity causes nearly all women (85 percent) and girls (79 percent) to opt out of important life activities, such as joining a club or class, voicing an opinion, or engaging with others.[10]

When comparing the confidence of girls and boys, researchers found no difference up until about the age of twelve. But in the tween and teen years, the confidence of girls plunges by 30 percent. They become "dramatically less self-assured." And all too often, this feeling persists.[11] The confidence gap stretches into adulthood. Women, on the whole, are markedly less self-assured than men.

A few years ago, information technology giant Hewlett-Packard commissioned a study to determine how to get more women into management positions. The authors discovered that male employees applied for promotions when they thought they could meet 60 percent of the job requirements. Women, on the other hand, only applied for promotions when they believed they met 100 percent of the job requirements. "So, essentially," Kay and Shipman concluded, "women feel confident only when we are perfect. Or practically perfect."[12]

Almost four out of five women, 78 percent, feel pressure to never make mistakes or show weakness.[13]

Study after study demonstrates that women are less likely to consider themselves competent, more likely to take criticism personally, and more likely to apologize for things that aren't their fault.

Lack of confidence is a widespread problem.

And it's a serious one.

The reason it's serious is that this negative trait doesn't usually hang out alone. It throws the door open and invites in a whole host of other unwelcome guests—like self-neglect, self-criticism, jealousy, attention-seeking, manipulation, people-pleasing, pessimism, perfectionism, anxiety, and depression.

People who struggle with confidence struggle a lot more at work and in their relationships. They have a tough time navigating life.

This is a significant issue we're talking about here.

The stakes are high.

Psychologists claim that a lack of confidence is at the root of most other problems. It's the common denominator they observe among clients, regardless of the reason the client initially sought help.[14]

A shortfall of confidence impacts us negatively in all sorts of ways. But the opposite is also true. A healthy dose of confidence comes with many positive benefits.

Confidence is linked to almost everything we want in life: success at work, secure relationships, a positive sense of self, and happiness. Confidence

- enables us to overcome insecurities,
- emboldens us to face our fears,
- equips us to succeed in relationships,
- energizes us to push through obstacles,
- empowers us to reach our potential,
- elevates us to achieve success, and
- endows us with peace and happiness.

Experts uphold confidence as the secret ingredient. They identify it as an essential element of internal well-being and a necessity for a fulfilled life. "With it, you can take on the world; without it, you live stuck at the starting block of your potential."[15] If only we could crack the "confidence code," then we'd get what our hearts desire.

It's clear that modern women are experiencing a pandemic of fear, anxiety, and insecurity. Popular authors claim that more self-confidence is the cure. But despite all the books and movies and positive messages, women are still struggling far and wide with confidence. Could it be there's something missing in these popular answers?

CRACKING THE CODE

The Bible has quite a lot to say about confidence problems. When God's people faced a daunting enemy, he advised them, "your strength will lie in quiet confidence" (Isa. 30:15 CSB). Apparently, quiet confidence was the trait that could make them strong. Confidence was the stuff they needed to outlast, outwit, and outplay their opponents.

King Solomon, the wisest man who ever lived, affirmed the importance of confidence in his collection of proverbs. He instructed his son, "The LORD will be your confidence and will keep your foot from being caught" (Prov. 3:26). Solomon knew that confidence would help his son succeed in life. It would prevent him from tripping up.

The prophet Jeremiah also emphasized the importance of confidence. He noted, "The person who trusts in the LORD, whose confidence indeed is the LORD, is blessed" (Jer. 17:7 CSB). *Blessed*, as you may know, means happy. Confident people are happy people.

David, whom the Bible identifies as a man after God's own heart, often sang about confidence. In fact, scholars even classify several of his psalms as "psalms of confidence."

"My heart is confident, God, my heart is confident," sang David (Ps. 57:7 CSB). "My heart is confident, God; I will sing; I will sing praises with the whole of my being" (Ps. 108:1 CSB).

David cracked the confidence code. His inner assurance would have been the envy of the women in the Lean In crowd. Evidently, he didn't need to read a self-help book or participate in a Lean In Circle to get to the place we all long to be.

Don't you wish you could have the kind of confidence he had? The kind that makes you break out into song and assuredly declare, "My heart is *confident*, God, my heart is *confident!*"

Interestingly, these verses confirm what modern research has discovered to be true. People who are confident are stronger, happier, and better able to navigate the challenges of life. The confidence gurus got that part right. But more importantly, these verses suggest that Scripture holds the key to cracking the confidence code. It's clear that confidence is a vital trait for God's people to possess and pursue. So, the question for you and me to consider is: What does God's brand of confidence look like, and how do we go about getting it?

TWO PARTS CAN-DO

I once heard confidence described as "one part sass and two parts can-do." What comes to mind when you hear the phrase *confident woman*? What qualities does such a woman possess? I pulled descriptions from articles and books. I also conducted a straw poll. Here's a summary of what most people think confidence entails. A confident woman:

- believes in herself,
- is independent,
- is competent,
- takes pride in her achievements,
- knows her own mind,
- has vision and drive,
- stands tall,
- carries herself with poise,
- dresses for success,
- voices her opinions,
- struts her stuff,
- acts like a boss,
- makes decisions with certainty,
- isn't intimidated,

- goes after what she wants,
- doesn't back down,
- questions the norm,
- takes risks,
- pushes for the top,
- portrays success,
- raises her hand,
- leans in.

If you hope to qualify as a role model of female confidence, you probably also need to be powerful, rich, and famous. The world attributes confidence to those who have made it to the top. Celebs like Sheryl Sandberg, JLo, or Kamala Harris, to name just a few.

So, if a woman exhibits all the qualities on the list, does that make her a confident woman? Is breaking the glass ceiling and making it to the top what confidence is all about? Apparently not. Because, as Kay and Shipman discovered, powerful women struggle with confidence just as much as you and I do. Just because they've mastered the art of speaking up and leaning in doesn't mean they've attained confidence.

And what about the woman who slouches, does not dress for success, doesn't have any stuff to strut, and isn't remotely interested in being the boss? Does her failure to live up to the pattern indicate that she lacks confidence? Just because she doesn't lean in or adopt a power stance, should we conclude that she's fraught with insecurity?

What about the woman who slops pigs on the farm? Or the one who flips burgers at McDonald's? Or what about the frail, arthritic granny in the nursing home? The idea that confidence requires a specified set of mannerisms and is restricted only to those in leadership positions puts confidence out of reach for women like this.

It seems to me that we need to scrap our preconceived notions, go back to square one, and come up with a working definition. What exactly is confidence? We can't hope to crack the code if we don't have a clear understanding of what it is we're after.

Most people regard confidence as a feeling: *I feel confident I can run that 5K in under forty minutes.* Confidence is equated with calmness, peace of mind, and faith that you'll succeed.

Sheryl Sandberg, for example, defines confidence as believing in your abilities.[16] Tony Robbins, the king of self-help, agrees: "Being confident is nothing more than a belief in yourself. It's the feeling of certainty that you can accomplish whatever you set your mind to."[17]

The problem with equating confidence with a feeling is that feelings don't always line up with our ability to face a challenge. People will tell you they feel confident when, inside, they're a quivering mess. Or the opposite. They'll tell you they feel they lack what it takes, then move forward with boldness. Who is the confident woman? The one who questions her ability but steps out and takes the risk anyhow? Or the woman who confidently boasts that she can do it but doesn't have the gumption to follow through?

Kay and Shipman argue that confidence is not just *feeling* good about yourself and *feeling* that you can do whatever you want.[18] It involves action—doing or thinking or even deciding, which is consistent with psychology professor Richard Petty's definition that "confidence is the stuff that turns thoughts into action."[19]

This definition touches on an aspect of confidence that's implied but not expressly addressed in the dictionary. Confidence is more than a feeling. It's more than a consciousness of power. It's an awareness of power that *moves us* to action. Confidence impacts what we do.

When we are confident, we are *compelled* by the power we sense we have at our disposal. We put our trust in that power. We step out in faith, believing it is enough for the task at hand. Confidence isn't just being aware of the power, like the guy who has a Ferrari parked in the garage but never takes it out for a drive. Confidence is an awareness of power that compels us to think, feel, and behave in a bold way.

The fact that confidence is the fuel for action becomes increasingly clear when we read through the list of words the thesaurus identifies as synonyms.

CONFIDENCE

Faith, Assurance, Certainty

Courage, Boldness, Backbone

Nerve, Daring

Fearlessness

Resolution, Determination

Tenacity, Fortitude

Pluck, Spunk

Grit[20]

The antonym of confidence is *diffidence*. You may not have heard that word before. It's an old-fashioned word that's largely absent from popular vernacular. Nowadays, most people use the word *insecure* instead. But *diffidence* is an important word to know when studying confidence. That's because confidence and diffidence are mirror opposites of each other.

Confident and *diffident* both trace back to the Latin verb *fidere*, which means "to trust." Both have to do with the amount of trust a person places in someone or something. The word *confident* adds the intensifying prefix *con-*, which means "plenty of," whereas *diffident* adds the prefix *dif-*, which means "the absence of."

Confidence means that someone has plenty of trust.

Diffidence means she has an absence of trust.

Both words have been used since about the fifteenth century and usually with reference to how much trust a person places in himself or herself. Confident people place plenty of trust in themselves. Diffident people don't. When it comes to their own ability, they lack trust.

DIFFIDENCE
(Lack of Confidence)

Doubt, Insecurity, Distrust

Reluctance, Hesitation

Cowardice

Shrinking back, Retiring

Flinching, Unassertive

Timidity

Fear[21]

Confident women are lionhearted; diffident women are mousy and sheepish. Confident women act in a bold manner; diffident women remain paralyzed by fear. Confident women dare; diffident women don't. Which type of woman would you rather be?

Um, the confident woman, Captain Obvious.

Of course you want to be a confident woman and not a diffident one! I want to be a confident woman. I want my daughters-in-law and my granddaughters to be confident women. I want my friends to be confident women. I want you to be a confident woman.

The question is, how? How do you transform your *can't-do* into a *can-do*? How do you turn your cowardice into bravery?

Telling a woman who feels diffident to "just be more confident" is like telling an emaciated refugee to "just eat more." It doesn't work. The refugee needs to find a safe haven and a good, reliable food source before she can sink her teeth into something that will satisfy her hunger.

We cannot deal with our lack of confidence by simply resolving to be more confident. Looking within—as self-experts advise us to do—is a nonsensical solution. The reason we're looking for more confidence is that those cupboards are bare.

CONFIDENCE IS TRUST

We've discovered that confidence comes from the Latin word which means "plenty of trust" or "firmly trusting." The concept of trust is central to the Bible's view of confidence. So central that it uses the words *trust* and *confidence* interchangeably.

For example, when Job's friend Eliphaz accused Job of relying on his great wealth rather than relying on God, Job vigorously denied the charge. Job claimed that he had never "made gold [his] *trust* or called fine gold [his] *confidence*" (31:24, emphasis added).

Interestingly, in this verse the Christian Standard Bible uses the word *confidence* where the English Standard Version uses the word *trust*, and *trust* where the other version uses the word *confidence*. Thus, in this second translation, gold is Job's *confidence* and fine gold his *trust*. Why the switcheroo? Did the translator get mixed up? No. The reason for the flip-flop word choice is that the Bible views *trust* and *confidence* as the same thing. The Hebrew words in this verse can be translated either way.

Confidence means trust. *Trust* means confidence.

There's something else super interesting about Job 31:24. Here, Job used a type of Hebrew poetry called parallelism. That means that the two lines mimic each other. The second line says the exact same thing as the first, albeit in a slightly different way. The parallelism reinforces the fact that making gold your trust and calling it your confidence mean the same thing.

Confidence means trust. *Trust* means confidence.

The first line in Job 31:24 does use a slightly different Hebrew word for trust/confidence than the second. This is also significant. The word in the first line, *kesel*, means "trust or confidence." The word in the second line, *mibtah*, means "the object of one's trust or confidence." Why is this significant? Because it indicates that the Bible views confidence and the object or source of that confidence as inseparably linked.

When Scripture speaks of confidence, it nearly always mentions the source of that confidence. In other words, rather than just talking in a general way about a person possessing confidence, as we so often do, the Bible usually indicates the thing in which the person is placing confidence.

For example, when the prophet Jeremiah rebuked the people of Moab, he didn't scold, "You were overly confident!" Instead, his reproach was, "You trusted [put confidence] in your works and your treasures" (Jer. 48:7).

Confidence doesn't occur in a vacuum. It's always attached to someone or something.

The dictionary defines *confidence* as "trust or faith in a person or thing."[22]

The Bible concurs.

But it has a distinct emphasis.

It is particularly concerned about which *person or thing* we are putting our *trust or faith* in.

CONFIDENCE IN CONFIDENCE ALONE

My oldest granddaughter, Clara, loves the classic 1965 film *The Sound of Music*. In the movie, Maria (Julie Andrews) panics when she leaves the safety of the abbey to go work as a governess for the von Trapp family. Though she's excited for the new adventure, she's overcome with doubts and worries about her ability to manage seven children. She breaks into a song—it is a musical, after all—to bolster her self-confidence and assure herself that she does, in fact, have what it takes.

As she makes her way from the abbey through the village to the von Trapp estate, she declares, "I have confidence the world can all be mine. . . . I have confidence in me." As the song continues, she reminds herself of all the things that contribute to her sense of confidence. She has confidence in sunshine. She has confidence in rain. She has confidence that spring will come again. As the song ends, Maria belts out this declaration: "All I trust I leave my heart to. All I trust becomes my own. I have confidence in confidence alone. Besides, which you see I have confidence in me!"[23]

The song is really quite insightful. It recognizes that we give our hearts to the things we place our confidence in. This reflects a truth expressed in the Bible. There is no clear line dividing our confidence from the source of our confidence. "All I trust becomes my own."

Maria's self-confidence is connected to her confidence in external sources. She even places confidence in "confidence alone." In other words, she chooses to have faith in the very concept of confidence. The whole mosaic of internal and external sources in which she places trust contributes to her declaration that she has "confidence in me."

Confidence is about who or what you trust. A woman could place trust in her own capabilities. Or she might place trust in her beauty, her possessions, her social standing, or her financial situation. She could place trust in another person, in the governing authorities, in her country's military power, or any number of other people or things. Like Maria in *The Sound of Music*, she could even put her confidence in the notion of being a confident woman.

Identifying confidence as coming from a specific source is largely absent from modern discussions about confidence. For example, let's say there's a nurse named Brittney who works in the cardiology ward of the local hospital.

Brittney is good at her job. Over the years she's climbed the ladder to become head nurse. Brittney is known for her knowledge, competence, decision-making skills, conscientious patient care, and also for standing up to medical residents and physicians—especially those who are condescending. Brittney assertively yet respectfully offers her opinion about the diagnosis and care of the patients in her ward. On more than one occasion, her intervention has even saved a patient's life.

Colleagues describe Brittney as self-confident. But that description doesn't really explain where Brittney's confidence comes from. Is Brittney confident because she has the right skills and experience? Because she trusts the expertise of the other health professionals on her team? Because she has access to all the latest cardiology equipment? Brittney's self-confidence can be based on a number of things.

Perhaps Brittney is a devout Christian. Perhaps she silently breathes a prayer as she goes about her work, asking the Great Healer to grant her wisdom. In that case, would it be inaccurate to say that Brittney has self-confidence?

Often, people will stick the word *self-* onto the front of the word *confidence* to indicate that they believe in their own capacity and not someone else's. They recognize that there's a difference between relying on an external source as the basis of one's confidence and relying on one's own inherent capabilities. But confidence and self-confidence can't be dissected quite so neatly. Internal and external sources of confidence are so enmeshed that they are virtually indivisible. As Maria noted, "All I trust becomes my own."

Consider this scenario: Nurse Brittney is proud to have earned her degree at a prestigious school. But what if the school's reputation were to be sullied in a massive public scandal? What if Brittney started to feel embarrassed about where she got her education? Though Brittney had nothing to do with her school's fall from favor, the event would surely impact the way she views her educational credentials. The external cannot be divorced from the internal. They're too intricately connected.

Most people use the words *confidence* and *self-confidence* interchangeably. To them, the two terms express the same concept. After all, whether Brittney draws confidence from her education, from her skills, from the coworkers she relies on, or from her relationship with God, the confidence is hers. Though self may not be the source of a woman's confidence, it is always the vessel for it. Even if you drop the *self-* from *confidence*, confidence is still connected to the self.

The tricky thing about the term *self-confidence* is that we have no way of knowing for sure whether a woman is trusting in self or in something else. Sometimes we can't even discern what it is we are actually trusting in. Our hearts can be deceitful.

I think of Belinda, a thirtysomething woman I met who was involved in a terrible car crash. Belinda was a marketing manager for a widget supply company. Though she was able to return to work after she recovered, she was left with a bad limp, a curled left arm, an eye that wouldn't open past half-mast, slurred speech, and the ongoing need to dab at the drool that so often dripped from the down-turned side of her mouth.

"If you would have asked me a few years ago whether I was putting my trust in my appearance, I would have given you an emphatic no," said Belinda. "I was never one to fuss about my appearance or obsess over the latest fashion. I would have told you that my confidence came from God alone." Belinda paused to dab at her mouth. Then she continued, "The accident revealed the idols of my heart. I realized just how much trust I was placing in other things. My appearance was one of them."

God wants you to be a self-confident woman, but not a woman who relies on self for confidence. The Bible's primary concern is that you place your confidence in God and not in lesser powers. When you have confidence in God, you will have all the self-confidence you need.

ALL I TRUST I GIVE MY HEART TO

The Old Testament uses four main Hebrew words for *confidence*. We came across two of them in Job 31:24. Although the four words are often swapped around and used interchangeably, they have slightly different shades of meaning:

CONFIDENCE

1. **BATAH:** to put trust/confidence in a person or thing
2. **MIBTAH:** the object of one's trust or confidence
3. **AMAN:** firmly based trust, strong confidence
4. **KESEL:** naive trust, foolish confidence

BATAH

The word *batah* means trust or confidence in a person or thing based on the presumed strength of that person or thing. The word carries overtones of firmness or solidity. *Batah* indicates that I feel safe, secure, or unconcerned. I feel a sense of well-being and security because I have something trustworthy on which I can depend.

Isaiah 12:2 is a good example: "Behold, God is my salvation; I will trust [be confident—batah], and will not be afraid; for the LORD GOD is my strength and my song, and he has become my salvation." The reason Isaiah felt confident was because he knew God was strong and reliable. Relying on God's strength made him feel safe, secure, unconcerned, and unafraid.

While it's undoubtedly true that God is strong and reliable, that may or may not be the case for other things in which we put our trust. Our presumption about the strength of something or someone may be wrong. Our confidence may be misplaced. For instance, Proverbs 11:28 warns that "whoever trusts [batah] in his riches will fall."

As you can see, *batah* talks about confidence in a general way, without giving any indication as to whether or not that confidence is well placed. I can place my confidence (batah) in God, but I can also place my confidence (batah) in things that will ultimately let me down.

MIBTAH

The next Hebrew word, *mibtah*, is closely related to *batah*. The main difference is that *batah* is used more like a verb, whereas *mibtah* is used more like a noun. *Batah* refers to the trust I place in something. *Mibtah* refers to the "something" in which I place my trust. That "something" actually *is* my trust.

For example, Proverbs 21:22 says a wise man scales the city of the mighty and brings down their mibtah. In this proverb, the sage is talking about the inhabitants of a city who had swag. They viewed themselves as mighty. Why? Because they had confidence in the strength of their city walls. The strength of the city made them feel safe and protected. There's a nuance in the original language that's lost in our English translations. They didn't merely *put* their confidence in the city. The city *was* their confidence.

Batah and *mibtah* refer to the confidence a person puts in a person or thing. But the words are neutral. They don't indicate whether that confidence is well placed—whether the object of confidence is strong and reliable or weak and unreliable. The final two Hebrew words, *aman* and *kesel*, provide more of an appraisal. These words give us hints about whether placing our confidence in something is a good idea. The evaluation is built right in.

AMAN

Aman means to put your confidence in something solid. It's firmly based trust or strong confidence. The word indicates that the object of your trust is genuinely capable, reliable, dependable, trustworthy, and true. You're smart to put your trust in that thing. Your confidence is well placed.

It will come as no surprise to you, then, that *aman* is most often used in the context of trusting the Lord. Over half its occurrences have to do with trusting or believing him. "[Abram] believed [aman] the Lord, and he counted it to him as righteousness" (Gen. 15:6).

Aman is the root from which we get the word *amen*. *Amen* has much more significance than just being the last word of a prayer. In Bible times, the response of "amen" after a statement was a means for worshipers to voice their agreement with what the speaker had just said.

Amen is an affirmation or endorsement that means, "Surely it is true!" or "Yes! You can be confident in this!" In modern emoji-speak, saying "amen" is like responding to a text with a string of thumbs-up symbols.

One of the names of God is *Elohim Amen*, "the God of Amen." This name of God indicates that he is faithful and true. He is rock solid. Trustworthy.

When we put our confidence in God, we are putting it in the right place.

KESEL

The final Hebrew word for confidence, *kesel*, means naive trust or foolish confidence. The word derives from a word that means foolishness and stupidity. It usually indicates that we are putting our trust in the wrong place.

I think you'll agree that we often naively put confidence in the wrong thing—whether it's our capability, education, job, finances, beauty, health, relationships, independence, freedom, political or economic stability, or any number of other things. Most of us have discovered that the things in which we place our confidence can fail and prove untrustworthy. The resulting pain, disappointment, and fear can be profound (COVID-19, anyone?).

The Hebrew words the Bible uses for confidence teach us quite a bit:

- We put trust or confidence in a person or thing based on what we presume to be the strength of that person or thing.
- The Lord is concerned about how strong the object of our confidence actually is.
- There's a right kind and a wrong kind of confidence. The right kind of confidence is reliance on something that's

trustworthy and strong. The wrong kind of confidence is reliance on something that's deceitful and weak.

Oh, how we need to learn to place our confidence in the right things . . . and not in things that will ultimately let us down.

A TALE OF TWO CONFIDENCES

If you are a logophile (someone who loves words), you probably have a copy of Charles Dickens's historical novel *A Tale of Two Cities* sitting on your shelf. The rest of us were forced to read this literary masterpiece in high school or college but weren't enamored enough to buy a copy, even though it is touted as the bestselling novel of all time.

Published in 1859, Dickens's classic tells the story of people who lived in London and Paris before and during the French Revolution. The book is perhaps best known for its oft-quoted opening line:

> It was the best of times, it was the worst of times, it was the age of wisdom, it was the age of foolishness, it was the epoch of belief, it was the epoch of incredulity, it was the season of Light, it was the season of Darkness, it was the spring of hope, it was the winter of despair, we had everything before us, we had nothing before us, we were all going direct to Heaven, we were all going direct the other way . . .[24]

Notice that this *long* opening sentence (and I didn't even quote the whole thing) is made up of a series of contrasts. Here, and throughout the rest of the book, Dickens made use of a literary technique called "antithesis." That's a fancy way of saying that he presented a contrasting set of thoughts or ideas that fall into two opposing categories.

It's the tale of *two* cities: London versus Paris, best versus worst, wisdom versus foolishness, belief versus incredulity, Light versus Darkness, hope versus despair, everything versus nothing, heavenward versus hellward.

In much the same way, the Bible sorts confidence into two opposing categories. It tells a tale of two confidences, so to speak. There's a right kind and a wrong kind. A strong kind and a weak kind. A smart kind and a stupid kind. A reliable kind and an unreliable kind. There's the kind that will hold you up and the kind that will let you down.

We could take Dickens's list of positive-negative contrasts and add the Hebrew words *aman* and *kesel* into the mix. When it comes to confidence, there's aman versus kesel, best versus worst, wise versus foolish, believing versus doubting, Light versus Darkness, hope versus despair, everything versus nothing, heavenward versus hellward, potent versus impotent, strong versus fragile. You get the idea.

The Bible, as a whole, contrasts the security of the type of confidence that comes from reliance on God with the folly of any other kind of security. The woman who puts her confidence in the Lord will be blessed and secure, whereas the woman who puts her confidence in other things is headed for a whole heap of hurt, disappointment, and trouble.

I want to introduce you to two verses that succinctly describe the Bible's two confidence categories:

1. **STRONG/SMART CONFIDENCE:** "In the fear of the LORD one has strong confidence" (Prov. 14:26).

2. **FRAGILE/FOOLISH CONFIDENCE:** "His source of confidence is fragile; what he trusts in is a spider's web" (Job 8:14 csb).

I'll be referring to these two verses several times throughout the rest of this book. We'll unpack them later. But for now, I just want you to notice that the Bible pits the type of confidence that is strong and smart against the type that is fragile and foolish.

What's more, as you may have deduced by now, the Bible's confidence code follows a distinct formula.

Are you ready for some math?

My daughter-in-law, Jacqueline, is an accountant. A math whiz. Me? Not so much.

Just a few years ago, during tax time, Jacqueline taught me that the numbers on my balance sheet were supposed to balance. Who knew?

Math is definitely not my strong suit. So, in order for me to "get it," I need an equation that's extremely simple. And thankfully, the formula for confidence is. It's easy enough for a grade-school student to understand. Here, in a nutshell, is the Bible's confidence code:

RELYING ON GOD > RELYING ON OTHER STUFF = STRONG/SMART CONFIDENCE
RELYING ON GOD < RELYING ON OTHER STUFF = FRAGILE/FOOLISH CONFIDENCE

Everything rests on the direction of that V-shaped symbol. The quality of my confidence depends on whether it's tipped to the left as a greater-than symbol (>) or to the right as a less-than symbol (<). The Bible teaches that when I depend on God *more* than (>) other things, I make a smart choice, and my confidence is strong. But if I depend on God *less* than (<) other things, I make a foolish choice, and my confidence is fragile.

Interestingly, the Bible's code for confidence is based on where I actually place my trust and not on my emotions; it doesn't matter how bold or fearful I may feel. I may possess all the positive energy and confidence in the world, but if my trust is misplaced, that confidence is foolish and fragile. On the other hand, even when I feel afraid, I can choose to embrace smart, strong confidence. As the psalmist declared, "When I am afraid, I will trust in you" (Ps. 56:3 CSB).

The world tells us that fear stands in the way of confidence. In order to gain confidence, we need to overcome fear. But Proverbs 14:26 seems to indicate that fear is the friend of confidence. "In the fear of the LORD one has strong confidence." So, which is it? Friend or foe?

If we want to tip that *V* in the right direction, we need to know a whole lot more about the relationship between confidence and fear.

2

FEAR IS YOUR FRENEMY

There is, after all, very grave cause for fear.

—Charles Spurgeon, "The Right Kind of Fear"

The bike was splendid! Vivid pink—dark-to-light ombré. Heart-shaped pedals. Filigree basket. Princess decals. Sparkles everywhere. Fully loaded.

When her mom showed her the listing on the buy-and-sell site, five-year-old Amery jumped up and down and squealed with delight. The snazzy-looking ride was my granddaughter's dream come true! She'd been asking for a bike for weeks. She could barely contain her excitement as she and her daddy drove to pick it up.

"Can I ride it yet? Can I ride it yet?" She badgered incessantly as Daddy adjusted the seat, lubricated the chain, and tightened the bolts on the sturdy training wheels. Finally, the bike was ready.

The whole family gathered for the big moment. Amery

confidently clambered onto the seat. It was perfect. Just the right size. Spectacular!

She beamed with pride as everyone cheered.

Obviously, it was time to take that gleaming jewel out for a spin. "Let's go to the playground!" Amery enthusiastically suggested. Callie led the way on her scooter. Mama followed close behind, pushing Joey in the stroller. Daddy and Amery were slated to bring up the rear.

But Amery's confidence faltered.

When it came right down to it, she was excited to sit on her new treasure, but she wasn't convinced that she could actually learn to ride it. Daddy assured her that the training wheels would hold her up. He held onto the bike and started to push from behind, encouraging her to pump her legs in circles following the direction of those pretty heart-shaped pedals.

Amery nervously giggled.

All was well . . . until Daddy let go . . . and the bike wobbled.

Amery shrieked in fear and scrambled off. No amount of assurance and coaxing and help from Daddy could convince her to get back on.

That darling bike is now gathering dust in the garage. And poor Amery is facing a common predicament.

She lacks confidence.

She badly wants to ride her bike but is just too afraid to do so.

FEARING FEAR

My granddaughter was confident she could ride a bike until fear got in the way. I'm sure that she'll eventually face her fear and triumph. (Just as she finally mustered up the courage to sleep on the top bunk in the bunk bed room at the lake.) She *will* get over it. She *will* learn to ride a bike. But for now, fear is definitely her enemy.

How often, as adults, do we face the same daunting opponent? We don't sign up, speak up, or stand up because we're too afraid. And just like my granddaughter and her princess bike, the magnitude of the fear that grips our hearts is often much bigger than the magnitude of the task at hand.

Fear is a powerful foe.

Remember the story of Gideon? The Lord instructed Gideon on how to defeat 135,000 Midianite warriors with only 300 men. It was obvious that the Midianite forces were vastly superior in number, strength, and military power. But when Gideon's men stood around the perimeter of the enemy camp one night, raised their torches, and blew their trumpets, the mighty army panicked. They turned on one another and fled.

What defeated the Midianite army?

Fear.

And then there's the story of the Syrian rout. King Ben-hadad had mustered his entire army to besiege Samaria, the capital city of the Northern Kingdom of Israel. He brought along about a quarter-million warriors—enough to populate a small city.

But when the rumor spread through Ben-hadad's vast camp that an alliance of Hittite and Egyptian mercenaries had come to the aid of Israel, the entire army fled in the middle of the night. They were so terror-stricken they left everything behind—horses, donkeys, tents, food, clothing, weapons, silver, gold. Everything.

What defeated the Syrian army?

Fear.

The rumor that sparked the panic wasn't even true.

Old Testament accounts indicate that the Lord often used

fear as a catalyst to compel the enemies of Israel to self-destruct. Massive, powerful armies were incapacitated—not by the power of weapons and chariots—but by the power of fear. "There they are, overwhelmed with dread, where there was nothing to dread," mocked the psalmist (Ps. 53:5 NIV).

These great armies were crushed by the enemy within. When fear gripped their hearts, they defeated themselves. From a purely human perspective, their fear was irrational. Unjustified. But that didn't matter. Irrational or not, it was fear that took them down.

In the sixteenth century, the great French writer Michel de Montaigne wrote about the debilitating nature of fear: "The thing in the world I am most afraid of is fear."[1]

He wasn't alone in fearing fear.

Franklin D. Roosevelt famously echoed the sentiment in his inaugural address. He told the American people that the only thing they had to fear was fear itself.

Roosevelt was alluding to the widespread fear that ushered in the Wall Street Crash of 1929 and became the hallmark of the ensuing Great Depression. Roosevelt recognized that the downward financial spiral would not end until people stopped being driven by fear and regained confidence in the market.

Fear is the enemy of confidence.

In order to gain confidence, we need a solid strategy to deal with this powerful foe.

WHAT'S TO FEAR?

The dictionary defines *fear* as "a distressing emotion aroused by impending danger, evil, pain."[2] We feel fear when we are faced with something out of our control that threatens to harm us—whether it endangers our physical, emotional, or psychological well-being and whether the threat is real or imagined.

Everybody fears something.

Common fears include the fear of flying, public speaking, heights, closed spaces, the dark, storms, spiders, needles, and death. And then, there are those general fears, which aren't always attached to a specific external object or event. Like the fear of failure, the fear of rejection, the fear of intimacy, the fear of commitment, or the fear of harm befalling someone we love.

The list of fears is virtually endless:

- fear of disapproval
- fear of disappointment
- fear of difficulty
- fear of exposure
- fear of embarrassment
- fear of exclusion
- fear of scarcity
- fear of sickness
- fear of success
- fear of being unnoticed
- fear of being unloved
- fear of the unknown

What scares you? What keeps you awake at night with worry? What stresses you out? Think about it for a moment. Perhaps you fear for your health, your safety, your job, your marriage, or your kids. Or maybe you're anxious about something that's going on in your school, church, community, or city. Recognizing what it is that you are afraid of is an important first step toward alleviating fear and gaining confidence. If you don't know what it is that scares you, you'll likely never do anything about it.

Fear can be sudden and intense or it can be persistent and dull. It can pounce on you unexpectedly or it can constantly escort you around. It can scream at you or it can nag. It can make you feel on edge or throw you into a full-blown panic attack. Fear comes in a whole range of shapes and sizes. Fear is so complex and multi-faceted that one online thesaurus identifies no less than 3,188 words as synonyms—part of the extended "fear family." Words like:

anxious • concerned • stressed
uneasy • nervous • apprehensive
scared • worried • frightened • freaked
fretting • quavering • shuddering • trembling
agitated • afraid • alarmed
disquieted • distressed • dismayed
dreading • despairing
panicked • horrified • terrified[3]

Simply reading the list is enough to make me feel uneasy. Fear is definitely a distressing emotion. We've all felt its icy fingers put a squeeze on our hearts.

One night I was home alone. My husband was out with friends. So, it was just me and my black lab, Sheba, curled up on the couch in the dark, watching TV.

Suddenly, I heard some movement outside on my back deck.

My heart started racing. My muscles tensed. My breathing sped up. My whole body kicked into crisis mode. The Queen of Sheba remained comatose, snoring at my feet. She is absolutely useless as a guard dog. Doesn't run to the door. Rarely ever barks. Obviously, it was up to me to defend our home. *What should I do?*

I quickly grabbed the cordless phone sitting on the coffee table and pressed 9 . . . 1 . . . Then I crouched down low, beneath the level of the windows, and stealthily crept through the darkness up the few steps to the main level of our house.

Every fiber of my body was on high alert.

I hunkered even lower as I made my way through the kitchen toward the open screen door. My stomach was tied in a knot. The blood pulsed in my head. My eyes squinted to make sense of the monochrome shadows. My ears strained to filter the TV dialog from the sound emanating from my deck. The hair on my arms stood on end. I tightly clenched the phone in my sweaty palm. My thumb rested on the dial pad, positioned to press the final number.

After what seemed like an eternity, I finally reached the switch for the outdoor light.

And abruptly flicked it on.

That's when my fear response abated . . . and the fear response of my neighbor's cat kicked in, causing her to loudly mew and bolt away.

That's also when the Queen of Sheba finally rolled off the couch and sauntered into the kitchen, yawning, stretching, and giving me her best "it's time for a treat" look.

Sigh. Time for some guard dog lessons, I say.

The sound I'd heard on the deck triggered an immediate and intense reaction. What I experienced was a classic fear response. I didn't consciously trigger it or even stop to analyze it until it had run its course. For those few seconds, I was so afraid that I reacted as if my life were in danger, even though there was really no danger at all.

Why is fear such a powerful emotion? Why does it produce such a strong response? Why can it motivate a weakling to stand up and fight? Or cause even the strongest, most competent person to cower and irrationally self-destruct?

HOW FEAR WORKS

Your brain has a fear system that involves four different circuits—all of which are activated at the same time. These circuits send signals back and forth to either inflame or dampen your feelings of fear. Let me explain how this fear system works.

1. ALARM CIRCUIT (AMYGDALA)

When you encounter a perceived threat—like a ferocious barking black dog running toward you (I guarantee it's not Sheba)—that threat causes your amygdala (the almond-shaped emotion-processing center in your brain) to send a distress signal to your hypothalamus (your system command center). The hypothalamus uses your nervous system to dispatch a body-wide code-red alarm.

A code-red alarm causes your pituitary gland to secrete a stress hormone into your blood and your adrenal glands to release a surge of adrenaline and cortisol. Energy is diverted away from your immune, reproductive, and digestive organs and redirected toward your brain, heart, lungs, and muscles. This increases your alertness and puts you into a heightened state of readiness. Most people call this the fight-or-flight response.

The alarm circuit is the brain's quick and messy way to respond to a crisis. My brain receives a signal of danger, and my body and emotions react without thinking—I instinctively jump, run, hide, scream, or grab the nearest object to use as a weapon. This reaction is automatic and involuntary.

The purpose of my alarm circuit is to fast-track my ability to protect myself from an imminent danger or threat. It is what causes me to slam on the brakes when the car in the other lane swerves into my lane. To jump when I hear a sudden loud noise. To gasp when a creepy-crawly drops onto my lap. Or to duck when an unexpected object comes flying at my head.

2. EVALUATION CIRCUIT (SENSORY CORTEX)

As your body is put on code-red alert, the hypothalamus also alerts and activates the second component of your stress response system: the sensory cortex. This part of your brain evaluates the information coming in through your senses and tries to make sense of it all.

I EVALUATE WHAT I HEAR: What is that noise? Is that a footstep? Is it the sound of a chair scraping against the deck? How far away is the sound from my door?

I EVALUATE WHAT I SEE: Is there something on my back deck? What is that dark shape? Is it a human shape? Is it moving?

I EVALUATE WHAT I SMELL: Is that cigarette smoke? Or a fire? Could my neighbor be outside grilling a steak at this hour?

The evaluation circuit works more slowly than the alarm circuit. While the alarm circuit puts my body on immediate alert just in case, the evaluation circuit has me gathering and appraising information to understand the situation.

3. ASSOCIATION CIRCUIT (HIPPOCAMPUS)

At the same time the alarm and evaluation circuits are firing, the hypothalamus alerts the hippocampus—your memory center—to instantaneously start going through your memory files. The hippocampus plays an important role in the formation and indexing of memories about experienced events. It works in concert with the amygdala to associate emotions with these events. The hippocampus compares the current event to past events to see if an association can be made.

Your brain subconsciously processes the situation, compares it with past experiences, and draws a conclusion, such as, *A situation like this harmed me before; it will undoubtedly harm me again.* Thus, if you were bitten by a dog, you may have a lifelong fear of dogs. If your father left your family, you may have a lifelong fear of abandonment. If you were bullied in grade school, you may have a lifelong fear of people laughing at you.

Humans learn to be afraid of dangerous things. But they can also learn to be afraid of things that aren't dangerous. There was an infamous behavioral experiment conducted in 1920 with a nine-month-old child called Albert. Researchers conditioned Albert to be fearful of white furry things—a white rat, a white bunny, a fluffy white dog, white stuffed animals, and a Santa Claus mask with a beard made of white cotton balls. The Little Albert experiment proved that given the right set of circumstances, people can learn to be afraid of virtually anything.

The thing that you're scared of is called a perceived threat. Perceived threats are different for each person. When you're faced with a perceived threat, your hippocampus informs your brain that you're in danger. It checks through your memory banks and concludes, based on past experience, that the situation is a threat to your well-being—whether it is or not. As a result, your body automatically reacts with the fight-or-flight response to keep you safe.

4. EXECUTIVE CIRCUIT (FRONTAL LOBE)

Have you ever heard the expression "She's afraid of her own shadow"? I once saw a YouTube video of a toddler who was. Apparently, she had never noticed her shadow before. When she spotted the spooky black figure standing next to her, she cried out in fear and tried to run away. Her cries and her fear intensified as the shadow followed her everywhere. Finally, she just collapsed in a puddle of helpless sobs. That's when her dad, who was chuckling as he caught the funny scene on video, turned off the camera.

I imagine that he went to pick her up and comfort her, to assure her that the shadow was cast by the sun shining on her body. There wasn't a spooky bogeyman chasing her. She had absolutely nothing to fear. In reasoning with her, her dad would have engaged her executive circuit, the final circuit in the human fear system.

The executive circuit is located in your frontal lobe. This is the largest part of your brain. The frontal lobe is responsible for thinking and decision-making. It is the part of the brain that takes charge. It is what you rely on to manage and modify your emotions and behavior.

Your executive circuit can either heighten or lessen your agitation. Depending on how you direct your thoughts, you can talk yourself into an increased or decreased state of fear.

Your alarm circuit and association circuit take what scientists call the "low road" to fear. This path is automatic and involuntary. Your evaluation and executive circuits take the "high road." This path is more deliberate and volitional. The low road is directed more by emotion while the high road is directed more by reason.

God created the low road and high road of fear to harmoniously work together. The low road warns us about a possibly dangerous situation. Then, the high road evaluates whether the threat is real and enables us to make a wise, volitional choice about the appropriate response. That's the way fear is *supposed* to work.

But we all know that fear can run amok.

Being put on the spot to give an impromptu speech can cause a bigger panic than encountering a bear. Walking into a room of strangers can induce more terror than a hurricane. A visit from your mother-in-law can throw you into more of a cold sweat than having your taxes audited by the IRS.

Our fear systems don't always cause us to respond in appropriate ways. Our alarm circuits can throw us into an irrational panic or keep us stuck in a perpetual state of anxiety. Our evaluation circuits can misinterpret evidence. Our association circuits can learn to fear the wrong things. And our executive circuits can be overruled by fearful emotions and render us helpless to respond in a reasoned way.

I think you'll agree that the reason fear is such a powerful and daunting enemy is that it distorts our perception of reality. Our fear is twisted. We don't fear as we should. We're afraid of things we shouldn't fear.

Fear itself can be our enemy.

It can be the reason for our self-destruction.

WHEN FEAR WENT AMOK

God created humans with an intricate built-in fear system. At the beginning, fear was an entirely helpful emotion. I imagine that Adam and Eve benefited from it as they went about their daily work in the garden. Adam's alarm circuit probably caused him to jump back when a pruned branch fell to the ground. His evaluation circuit informed him that it hurt to have a big branch fall on his toes. His association circuit made him more wary the next time he took his tools out to prune branches. His executive circuit advised him that he should stand back and take all the necessary precautions when working overhead to avoid getting hurt.

Fear taught the first couple to have a healthy respect for fire, water, light, dark, height, weight, mass, and things like the force of friction, the force of gravity, the power of momentum, and all the other natural laws that God wove into the universe. Fear informed them that these things were bigger than they were and driven by forces beyond their control. Fear taught them they could not defy the natural laws of God without risk of injury.

Fear served Adam and Eve in other ways too. The Bible indicates that, in addition to equipping them with an innate response system that helped protect them from physical danger, God created another kind of fear to reside within their hearts—the fear of God. This reverent fear helped protect them from spiritual danger. We'll unpack what that means later, but for now, just think of the fear of the Lord as a deep awe and worshipful respect for our Creator and a sense of our own creaturely dependence on him. Fearing God entails a proper perspective of who he is and who we are in relation to him. He is God, and we are not.

It's similar to the type of fear that a child has for a loving father. She's not afraid of her dad in the sense of distrusting him. She's not worried that he will be unloving, cruel, or unjust, or that he will harm her. Her fear is a trust-based respect of his wisdom, strength, protection, and position of authority in the family. This type of fear benefits her. It motivates her to respectfully listen to her father's instruction, to believe what he tells her, and to do what he says.

That's the healthy kind of fear that Adam and Eve initially had toward the Lord. That is, until the sneaky talking Serpent convinced them to entertain a completely different kind of fear.

You know the story.

Using deceit and shrewd double-talk, the Serpent introduced a completely new kind of fear into Eve's mind. *Did God really say . . . ?* (Gen. 3:1 csb). On the surface, the friendly talking reptile was just discussing the rules of the garden and the merits of the fruit that God had labeled off-limits. But on a deeper level, the conniver was baiting Eve to have deep misgivings about God.

Misgivings. Suspicion. Unease. Concern. Disquietude. Doubt. Worry.

Where have we seen these words before? They are all part of the fear family. They aren't nearly as flashy, extreme, or forcible as their family members *panic, horror,* and *dread.* Had the Serpent used a heavy-handed approach, Eve's amygdala would have thrown her alarm circuit into a full-blown fight-or-flight response. That wouldn't have served his purpose at all. But the devil knew that fear is a powerful motivator of human behavior. So he activated her fear network using a much more devious approach.

With half-truths that could fool even the best con artist, he filled her thoughts with low-grade, snaky, nagging suspicions and fears that

- God wasn't telling the truth,
- God wasn't as good as she thought,
- God didn't have her best interests at heart,
- God was holding her back,
- she was missing out, and
- trusting God was a terrible mistake.

The sneaky Serpent implied that God posed a legitimate threat to Eve's personal development and well-being. What's more, he nudged her to confidently act against that threat. He convinced her that she should take matters into her own hands.

She could confidently stand on her own two feet! She could reach out and take what she wanted! She could set aside the silly reverent fear of God that was holding her back! Success was within her power and grasp.

Essentially, Eve had to choose which fear was going to control her behavior—the reverent fear of the Lord that was part of her created design or the nagging apprehensive fear the Serpent had introduced into her mind.

What the Serpent said seemed to make sense. The forbidden fruit did look good.

It looked attractive. Alluring. Beautiful. It was a "delight to the eyes" (v. 6).

It appeared harmless. Tasty and delicious. It seemed "good for food" (v. 6).

It held such promise. It was "desired to make one wise" (v. 6).

Anybody who wanted to be somebody would surely take a bite.

If the fruit hadn't seemed so appealing, do you think Eve would have fallen for the offer? If it had been rotten and crawling with worms, do you think she would have considered disobeying God? Of course not. What makes Satan's offers so alluring and so deceptive is that they always look so good. The fruit looked attractive, harmless, and promising, so . . .

She took.

She ate.

She gave.

He took.

He ate.

Adam and Eve embraced the distorted, lie-based fear promoted by Satan. In doing so, they rejected the truth-based fear that had been the foundation of their love relationship with the Lord.

That's the moment fear fell through the looking glass and started to run amok.

The change was immediate.

Imagine the sheer force of emotion that must have overwhelmed Adam and Eve when they sinned and their innocence was destroyed. It must have been horrifying. The shame. The overwhelming sense of grief and loss. For the first time ever, they felt embarrassed. Damaged. Unsafe. Exposed. Truly afraid.

Satan leveraged Eve's fear system to get her to act against God. But the low-grade concern that caused her to doubt God was nothing compared to the terror that now gripped her and her husband's hearts. Losing their reverent fear of God opened the floodgates to all sorts of apprehensive fears. In panic, they tried to sew some fig leaves together in a pitiful attempt to cover themselves up.

When God came to the garden that night, Adam and Eve were nowhere to be found. Adam later explained, "I heard the sound of you in the garden, and *I was afraid*, because I was naked, and I hid myself" (Gen. 3:9–10, emphasis added).

Adam was afraid because he realized he was naked. Eve was gripped with the same fear.

They didn't say they were afraid of God's judgment. They didn't say they were afraid that they had let him down. They didn't say they were afraid he might respond in anger. They didn't say they were afraid of the consequences of their sin.

No. They were afraid because they didn't want God to see them in their birthday suits.

Think about that for a moment.

Isn't it a tad irrational?

To that point, they had never been anything but naked. Since the day God created them, they had walked around nude. Their private parts were always on full display. It seems silly that they would suddenly be afraid of him seeing them naked. That fear was misplaced. Absurd. Nonsensical.

Of course, we know that their panicked impulse to cover up was really an attempt to hide their guilt. But this fearful reaction indicates that their view of God had radically changed. Their positive fear had been replaced with a negative one. They feared embarrassment. They feared exposure. They feared that God would see them for who they really were.

Did they really think that God didn't know what they had done? Did they think that he couldn't see through their pitiful attempt to cover their sin? Why did they slink away from him instead of running toward him? Had he ever given them reason to distrust his compassion? Or to doubt his love?

Sewing themselves leafy aprons was more than just an attempt to alleviate their shame. It reflected a sense of self-reliance, self-justification, and self-determination. It was another expression of the overconfident attitude that had gotten them into trouble in the first place.

Up until that point, Adam and Eve had only known God to be loving, kind, and good. Now they were afraid of him. What had happened? Had God changed? No. But they had. Sin changed them. It affected their view of him and who they were in relation to him.

One of the most devastating effects of sin is that it distorted Adam and Eve's fear system. They lost their healthy fear of God. Illegitimate, irrational, lie-based fears began to dominate their minds and behavior.

Before the fall, fear served a wholly good and protective

purpose. It kept humans physically and spiritually safe. After the fall, fear began to serve an evil and destructive purpose. It became a powerful tool of the Enemy. Ever since that fateful day, Satan has relentlessly used fear as a weapon against us.

CONFIDENCE ARTIST

Fear is the feeling that something is more powerful than I am and beyond my control. Fear introduces uncertainty and apprehension. It diminishes my confidence. I evaluate the threat and conclude, *I don't have what I need to face this situation.*

When I feel fear, I look for a way to alleviate the uneasy emotion. I can run away from the threat, or I can look for another person or thing in which to place my trust in order to diminish fear and regain confidence.

Fear and confidence are both powerful motivators of human behavior.

Robert Plutchik, a psychologist renowned for his theory of emotions, identified fear and trust as two of the eight primary emotions at the core of our human emotional makeup. The big eight are: fear, trust, joy, anticipation, anger, disgust, sadness, and surprise.[4]

Marketers understand the power of appealing to these eight core emotions when promoting a product—especially the powerful emotions of anticipation (hope), fear, and trust.

That Gleam & Sparkle toothpaste ad isn't just selling you toothpaste. It's pitching the message that this toothpaste will remove the ugly stains from your enamel (disgust), help you overcome your insecurities (fear), attract the man of your dreams (anticipation), and make you happy (joy). You can be confident (trust) that just as the tried-and-true Gleam & Sparkle brand did this for Ms. Hot Celebrity, it will surely do it for you. It's a limited-time offer. You had better stop what you're doing and purchase some Gleam & Sparkle toothpaste. Don't delay. Do it now!

We know that companies use emotional marketing to sell their products. We also know that hustlers leverage our emotions for much more sinister purposes. Take the tech-support pop-up scam, for instance. In this scam, a pop-up message appears on your computer screen from a well-known software company, like Microsoft, Apple, Norton, or Dell. The message claims that the company has detected a virus or that your computer is about to crash, causing a massive loss of data. They offer to fix the problem and repair your computer for a fee.

You feel fearful. *Something is wrong with my computer? A virus?! Oh no!* You feel relieved that someone with more computer knowledge than you is able to help. You trust the legitimacy of the company sporting the familiar logo. You hope that they will be able to fix the problem and send you on your way with a computer that is virus-free and running better than ever.

Tech-support scammers want you to pay for services you don't need to fix a problem that doesn't exist. How do they do this? They lie. They craft a deceitful scenario to leverage your fears and convince you to put your trust in them.

Have you ever been tricked by a phone call or text or email, or by someone you met online, only to find out later that you had been scammed? I was once taken in by an email from Apple that appeared real but turned out to be fake. I had to spend hours online with Visa in the middle of our vacation to reverse the charges the swindler had racked up on my account.

Perhaps you've never fallen for a financial scam.

But I know you've fallen for a spiritual one.

We all have.

Satan is the master con artist. As the Bible explains in John 8:44, "[The devil] does not stand in the truth, because there is no truth in him. When he tells a lie, he speaks from his own nature, because he is a liar and the father of lies" (CSB).

Satan is a pathological liar. He's the biggest fraudster, swindler, scammer, and victimizer of all. He's a thief who comes only to steal and to kill and to destroy. He is more highly skilled at duplicity, cajolery, manipulation, and persuasion than any con artist that has ever lived. And he's constantly trying to leverage our fears and insecurities to sell us a bill of goods.

Let me remind you that the *con* in con artist is short for *confidence*. A con artist convinces you to put your confidence in him and in his amazing promises. He plays con games—confidence games—to win your confidence.

I once watched an online interview with a top Washington fraud investigator. He said that a con artist's central strategy is to get his victims "under the ether" by bypassing their reason and appealing to a deep fear or desire.[5]

When Satan talked to Eve about the forbidden fruit, he was essentially engaging her in a confidence game. The expert hustler played on Eve's emotions to undermine her trust in the Lord and scam her into placing her confidence in him instead. According to Satan, all she had to do to alleviate her nagging fears and realize her dreams was to bite into the forbidden fruit.

It was a sham, of course. Biting into the forbidden fruit didn't make Eve's dreams come true. The ether wore off—and the horrible pain set in. It produced appalling consequences—in her body; in her mind, will, and emotions; in her relationship with God; and in her marriage. Adam and Eve's sin resulted in ugly, destructive consequences for every human who has ever lived.

And one of the most disastrous effects was the shift in what we naturally fear and where we naturally place our confidence.

CONFIDENCE GAME

Satan engaged Eve in a devious confidence game. His goal was to make her fear the wrong things, put her confidence in the wrong things, and desire the wrong things.

Do you remember the formula for confidence from the last chapter?

RELYING ON GOD > RELYING ON OTHER STUFF = STRONG/SMART CONFIDENCE
RELYING ON GOD < RELYING ON OTHER STUFF = FRAGILE/FOOLISH CONFIDENCE

Before Eve sinned, she possessed strong, smart confidence. She relied on the Lord more than she relied on other things. Trusting God was her natural bent. But then Satan tricked her into flipping the direction of the *V*. When she bit into the fruit, her bent changed. She began to place more confidence in Satan's twisted version of reality than in what God said. She turned her back on strong, smart confidence and embraced fragile, foolish confidence instead. And humans have continued to do so ever since.

To this day, the great Con Man continues to play the same confidence game. He continues to use the same tactics that he effectively used on our foremother, Eve.

THE CONFIDENCE MAN PEDDLES FEAR

Satan is a fearmonger. He promotes insecurity, doubts, anxieties, despair, and all the other destructive parts of the fear family. He cons us into fearing things we shouldn't fear. We fear that God isn't big enough, good enough, or that he doesn't care. We fear that God won't come through the way we want him to. We fear people. We fear exposure. We fear disapproval. We fear failure. We fear loss. We fear all sorts of things.

Most of our fears are based on Satan's twisted version of reality and the lies he perpetuates. Nevertheless, these fears erode our confidence. They cripple us and keep us locked in a state of anxiety, stress, defeat, and despair. Of course, we want to alleviate all those uneasy, fearful emotions. So, we search for something in which to place our trust in hopes of diminishing fear and increasing our confidence.

THE CONFIDENCE MAN PEDDLES CONFIDENCE

In the same way the pop-up tech-support scammers offer a solution for a problem they themselves created, Satan sells us his bogus snake oil remedies. He not only peddles fear but also peddles fragile, foolish confidence as a supposed cure. He's satisfied as long as our confidence V is tipped in the right direction—away from God.

Satan is God's archenemy. He loathes God. And he is eager to have us join him in his cosmic rebellion. As was the case with Eve, Satan is especially interested in encouraging our self-reliance and self-determination. When we buy into his scheme, we place more confidence in our competence and know-how—or in our own appearances, likability, money, possessions, friends, or abilities—than we place in the One who gives us these things.

Does Satan want you to be confident? You bet he does. As long as you are confident in anything and everything except God.

THE CONFIDENCE MAN PEDDLES TRUST

Satan holds out a basket of tasty-looking fruit and invites us to partake. He dupes us into trusting that his ways are better than God's ways. As he did with Eve in the garden, he convinces us that the forbidden fruit is attractive. Harmless. Delicious. It holds such promise!

Satan tries to get us under the ether in countless ways. He seeks to convince us that the pleasure and the benefits we will receive from doing it his way instead of God's way are worth any potential consequences. And although we know—intellectually—that these things are sin, the ether, the delusion and deception of the huckster's promised benefits, motivates us to shrug our shoulders and confidently indulge.

Ever since mankind fell, people have been born under the ether, with an innate disposition to fall for the great swindler's lies.

But thankfully, that's not the end of the story.

FAITH CRUSHES FEAR

Adam and Eve were still cowering in their fig leaves when God spoke of a deliverer who would one day conquer the power of the fearmongering Serpent.

God warned the Serpent, "I will put hostility between you and the woman, and between your offspring and her offspring. He will strike your head, and you will strike his heel" (Gen. 3:15 CSB). Eve and her adversary were the progenitors of a fear-based struggle that would continue throughout history until the climactic moment when the woman's offspring would achieve the upper hand.

Theologians call this verse the "protevangelium"—the first telling of the gospel—because it's the first place in the Bible that announces the good news of the coming Savior, Jesus Christ. Paul alluded to this promise when he assured his friends, "The God of peace will soon crush Satan under your feet" (Rom. 16:20).

Did you notice the name Paul used for God? The God of Peace.

Through Jesus, God crushes Satan. Peace crushes panic. Faith crushes fear.

The consistent message of the Bible is that when we put our confidence in God, we don't need to be afraid of other people, circumstances, or things. When we have strong confidence, the right kind of confidence, we can beat Satan at his double-dealing confidence game.

When you boil it right down, our struggle against fear and apprehension is essentially a struggle to place our confidence in the right thing instead of the wrong thing. It's the age-old struggle to believe God's truth rather than Satan's lies.

It's a difficult battle.

Tough.

Lifelong.

Relentless.

Our struggle against fear is as persistent and ongoing as our struggle against sin. Yet the battle is not without hope. And we are not left without help. God says:

> Fear not, for I am with you;
>> be not dismayed, for I am your God;
> I will strengthen you, I will help you,
>> I will uphold you with my righteous right hand. . . .
> For I, the LORD your God,
>> hold your right hand;
> it is I who say to you, "Fear not,
>> I am the one who helps you." (Isa. 41:10, 13)

The Bible assures us that with God on our side, we have no reason to fear. We can embrace confidence because the Lord is bigger than anything that threatens to harm us.

FEAR IS YOUR FRIEND

It's undeniable that there is a close connection between fear and confidence. Generally speaking, increased fear results in decreased confidence; increased confidence results in decreased fear. That's why "how to build confidence" articles tend to dispense this sort of advice:

> Self-confidence is belief in yourself. It is your ability to trust your abilities. The reason for lack of self-confidence can almost always be summed up in one word: *fear*. This could be fear of embarrassment, fear of rejection, fear of criticism, fear of failure, or one of many other kinds. Fortunately, all fears are learned. No one is born with fears. Fears can, therefore, be unlearned by practicing self-discipline repeatedly with regards to fear until it goes away and one becomes more confident.[6]

This quote sums up what most people believe to be true: Fear is bad. Fear is the archenemy of confidence.

Therefore, the key to building confidence is to conquer fear.

If you would only face your fear—stare it down until fear becomes your slave and you its master—then you would gain a greater trust in your abilities. Defeating fear is how to grow more confident.

The Bible's instruction on how to grow more confident doesn't exactly follow this popular formula. It positions the fear of the Lord against other fears.

When you fear God more, you fear other things less. And when your fear of these other things is reduced, you have more of the right kind of confidence. Therefore, if you want your confidence to increase, your fear of God needs to increase.

What? How can that be? Isn't fear the problem? Isn't confidence about alleviating my fears? I have plenty of fear. What I really need is less fear, not more!

The Bible's path to confidence is counterintuitive. Just as there is a wrong and a right kind of confidence, there is a wrong and a right kind of fear. And Scripture indicates that the way to combat the former is with the latter. The way to fight fear is with fear of a different kind.

Our strong, smart confidence category verse in Proverbs 14 makes the connection between holy fear and strong confidence clear:

> In the fear of the LORD one has strong confidence,
>> and his children will have a refuge.
> The fear of the LORD is a fountain of life,
>> that one may turn away from the snares of death.
> (vv. 26–27)

There are a few things I want you to notice in this passage. First, the fear of the Lord is a refuge—both for the person who fears God and for his or her children. What is a refuge? It's a place of shelter, protection, or safety. A refuge keeps us safe from harm. A refuge is a place that alleviates fear. The fear of the Lord is a refuge that cancels out other fears.

Second, the fear of the Lord is a fountain of life. It's nourishing. Life-giving. Healthy. Wholesome. Good. It's the opposite of the poisonous, deceptive, destructive fear that Satan promotes.

Third, the fear of the Lord empowers us to turn away from the snares of death. In other words, a holy, reverent fear frees us from being entrapped by the confidence schemes of the great swindler, Satan.

Finally, and most notably, in the fear of the Lord you will find strong confidence. It's important for you to understand this vital point: *The fear of God is what will transform you into a strong, confident woman.*

There's one more simple confidence code equation I'd like to add to our formula. In the first chapter, we discovered that relying on God more than relying on other stuff is what produces strong, smart confidence. To that we might add: fearing God more than fearing other stuff is what produces strong, smart confidence.

RELYING ON GOD > RELYING ON OTHER STUFF = STRONG/SMART CONFIDENCE
FEARING GOD > FEARING OTHER STUFF = STRONG/SMART CONFIDENCE

The Bible is clear that people who put their faith in God through Jesus Christ have a markedly different relationship to fear than people who don't. As believers, our lives are directed by holy fear. We fear God; therefore, we're not afraid of other things. We don't fear people. We don't fear sickness or death. We don't fear failure, embarrassment, or loss. We don't fear the things that other people fear. (At least, with God's help, we're learning not to.)

Unbelievers are helpless against the schemes of the fearmongering Con Man.

If you don't trust in God, then you're putting your faith in Satan's false narrative. Your life is directed by unholy fear. You don't fear God; therefore, you *are* afraid of other things. And although you try your best to drum up enough self-confidence to alleviate your anxieties, doubts, and insecurities, deep down you know it's a losing battle.

The prophet Isaiah learned that he needed to have a markedly different relationship to fear than people who weren't following the Lord:

> For the LORD spoke thus to me with his strong hand upon me, and warned me not to walk in the way of this people, saying: "Do not call conspiracy all that this people calls conspiracy, and do not fear what they fear, nor be in dread. But the LORD of hosts, him you shall honor as holy. Let him be your fear, and let him be your dread." (Isa. 8:11–13)

Isaiah was facing a stressful situation. He was likely being accused of conspiracy because he opposed Israel's alliance with Assyria, an alliance that transgressed God's clear instructions. By leveling an accusation of conspiracy against him, detractors hoped to pressure and intimidate Isaiah into shutting up. Their fearmongering tactics had worked on most of the population, and they hoped they could also scare Isaiah into agreement—or at least into silence.

The Lord warned Isaiah not to fear the things that others feared. Others were afraid of standing up against the celebrities of the day and against popular opinion. They were afraid of being shamed, shunned, and perhaps of being socially, economically, or legally sanctioned.

Isaiah was not to fear what they feared. He was not to dread what they dreaded. The Lord told him that he needed to keep his fear in the right place: *Let the Lord be your fear. Let him be your dread.*

God's point was that Isaiah needed to fight fear with fear. Fearing God would help him fear other things less. Fearing God would increase his confidence.

The Lord often took his people to task for fearing other things more than they feared him (Isa. 57:11). Jesus likewise warned, "I tell you, my friends, do not fear those who kill the body, and after that have nothing more that they can do. But I will warn you whom to fear: fear him who, after he has killed, has authority to cast into hell. Yes, I tell you, fear him!" (Luke 12:4–5).

You see, the Lord wants to put fear and confidence back in their proper place—the place they occupied before sin messed everything up. God wants to crush the negative, apprehensive, lie-based fear that is such a powerful tool of the Enemy and reinstate the positive, reverent, truth-based fear that originally existed in the human heart. He sent Jesus Christ, the Prince of Peace, to accomplish this. "The reason the Son of God appeared was to destroy the works of the devil" (1 John 3:8).

That's good news. Exceptionally good news!

And it has profound implications for the way you deal with your fears and insecurities. The aim is not that you would stop being controlled by fear but that you would stop being controlled by the wrong kind of fear and start being controlled by the right kind of fear.

Fear is your frenemy. The wrong kind of fear is a confidence killer—the right kind of fear is a confidence builder. The wrong kind of fear is your enemy—the right kind of fear is your friend.

3

HELLO, MY NAME IS FEAR

> Where [fear] reigns it produces a holy security and
> serenity of mind. There is in it a *strong confidence*.
>
> —Matthew Henry, Proverbs 14:26–27 Bible commentary

Her name was Fear. Fear Brewster. She was born in Nottinghamshire, England, in 1606. Her family was among the first settlers of the Plymouth Colony of New England, on the shores of Cape Cod Bay in present-day Massachusetts.

Fear? Who would give their daughter such a name? And why? It seems thoughtless. Cruel, even. Imagine going through life writing FEAR in capital letters in every first-name blank on every form. Having your homeroom teacher call out, "Fear? Fear, are you here?" while taking attendance each morning. And introducing yourself to strangers at dinner parties saying, "Hello. My name is Fear." It would be awkward. Embarrassing.

Fear is such an unbecoming name. It's true that some celebrity baby names make us stop and scratch our heads. (I doubt that any of your friends named their child Apple or Blanket.) But even celebrities generally avoid names with negative connotations. Naming a child Fear seems akin to naming her Morbid, Witless, or Coward. Who would do that?

Fear's father, William Brewster, doesn't strike me as the type who would have given his child a silly name. He studied at Cambridge University and was educated in both Greek and Latin. He was a prominent leader of the Puritans who immigrated to the New World on the *Mayflower* in 1620.

As the only university-educated member of the Plymouth community, Brewster is credited by historians with drafting the Mayflower Compact, a set of rules for the governance of the new colony. By virtue of his close association with his friend, the governor William Bradford, he played a major role in civil as well as religious affairs.

Why would such a highly respected man name his daughter Fear? And why would his wife go along with it?

Some historians claim that she was named Fear because at the time of her birth, the Puritans were holding illegal church services. It was the "constant 'fear' of arrest due to this then-illegal activity which inspired them to bestow this unfortunate name upon their daughter."[1]

It's true that the Brewsters' lives were difficult. They were Separatists, part of a group of Christians who refused to pledge allegiance to the Church of England. Due to their religious convictions, the Brewsters boycotted state-run church services and hosted worship services in their manor instead. For this crime, William Brewster and other church leaders were arrested and sent to jail.

Upon release, Brewster led the Puritan migration to Holland in hopes of escaping religious persecution. There, he printed and sold Puritan books that had been banned by the English government. King James exerted pressure on Dutch authorities to rearrest him. But Brewster escaped. Shortly thereafter, he sailed across the ocean with the Puritans to establish a new colony. His dream was to raise his family in a land that supported freedom of religion and liberty of conscience.

William Brewster was a brave, bold man. It wasn't fear of persecution that motivated him and his wife to give their daughter such an odd name. No. It was because the Puritans believed that fear was central to the Christian experience and essential for bold, godly living.

The website Oh Baby! Names mocks the name Fear. It quips, "Fear Brewster is probably the only creature on earth to have been given such an ill-fated name."[2]

Actually, Fear Brewster wasn't the only girl named Fear. Her paternal aunt bore the same name. Other women in the Puritan community likely did too. That's because the Puritans upheld fear as a rare treasure—a beautiful and desirable thing. To them, the name pointed to something just as valuable, precious, and appealing as the name Hope or Grace.

POSITIVELY ARCHAIC

It comes as no surprise that people nowadays would consider the name Fear to be "ill-fated." After all, most of us solely think of fear as the strong and unpleasant emotion we feel when we think that we are in danger. Fear is a negative feeling we generally want to avoid.

Some dictionaries acknowledge that fear has another definition. It can also mean "to regard God with reverence and awe." But those dictionaries usually label this alternate meaning as "archaic." Oxford University Press, for example, defines fear this way:

fear, *noun*

1. An unpleasant emotion caused by the threat of danger, pain, or harm. "I cowered in fear as bullets whizzed past."
1.1 (fear for): A feeling of anxiety concerning the outcome of something or the safety of someone. "Police launched a hunt for the family amid fears for their safety."
1.2 The likelihood of something unwelcome happening. "She observed the other guests without fear of attracting attention."
1.3 *archaic* A mixed feeling of dread and reverence. "The love and fear of God."[3]

The *archaic* label indicates that the definition of fear as a mixed feeling of dread and reverence—as in the fear of God—is now defunct. Although people from a bygone era viewed fear that way, modern-day people do not. The editor of the dictionary wants you to know that you shouldn't be using this definition because it's old-fashioned and on its way out the back door.

If you were to crack open a dictionary from the 1800s, though, you would see that people of that day did indeed view reverence as a legitimate—and even prominent—meaning of fear.

Noah Webster, a descendant of Governor William Bradford of Plymouth, published the famous *Webster's Dictionary* in 1828. It contained nine entries for the definition of the noun *fear*. Almost all of the entries referred to the Bible in one way or another. Here are the final four:

fear, *noun*

6. In scripture, *fear* is used to express a filial or a slavish passion. [Filial *fear*] In good men, the *fear* of God is a holy awe or reverence of God and his laws . . . ["That they may *fear* me forever" (Jer. 32:39, emphasis added)].
Slavish *fear* is the effect or consequence of guilt; it is the painful apprehension of merited punishment. Romans 8:15 ["For you did not receive the spirit of slavery to fall back into fear"].
7. The worship of God. . . . Psalms 34:7 ["The angel of the LORD encamps around those who fear him."]
8. The law and word of God. "The *fear* of the LORD is clean, enduring forever" Psalms 19:9.
9. Reverence; respect; due regard. "Render [therefore] to all their dues: [. . .] *fear* to whom *fear*." Romans 13:7.[4]

The meaning of fear has definitely changed. A large part of the original meaning has been lost and is now viewed as archaic. In modern-day usage, the word is quite one-dimensional. It simply means feeling scared and apprehensive about something. In the past, however, the word had a much broader meaning. It meant not only apprehension but also reverence, awe, worship, respect, and due regard.

When people of past generations heard the word *fear*, a much richer, multidimensional concept came to mind—a notion that is actually more in line with the Bible's definition.

In the Bible, the word *fear* can indicate that someone feels scared and apprehensive. But Scripture most often sets this negative type of fear up against a positive type of fear. It gives the positive type of fear significantly more emphasis and presents it as being far more powerful than the negative type. In fact, it teaches that the way to overcome debilitating fear is with more fear—fear of a positive, empowering kind.

A FAMILY TREASURE

It's tragic that people have lost an appreciation for the positive dimension of fear. I can't help but think that the reason why women today struggle so much with confidence is that we have an incomplete view of what fear is all about. We've forgotten the fear of the Lord.

If strong confidence is found in the fear of the Lord, as the Bible says it is, then we must embrace that kind of fear in order to become strong, confident women.

John Bunyan, a seventeenth-century English writer and Puritan preacher, best known for his allegory *The Pilgrim's Progress*, viewed fear as a great gift. He called fear a "blessed grace."[5] According to Bunyan, this blessed grace of fear is a darling grace, a godly jewel, a choice jewel, and a priceless treasure. It "makes men excel, and go beyond all men in the account of God; it is that which beautifies a man."[6]

Fear is a blessed grace, a darling grace . . . a choice jewel . . . a priceless treasure . . . Fear can raise you up and make you excel beyond others . . . Fear beautifies you.

Have you ever heard anyone say these kinds of things about fear?

Have you ever known anyone who cherished and embraced fear this much?

What's particularly interesting is that Bunyan's delight in the fear of God enabled him to live so fearlessly. He boldly preached the good news, even though he knew it was illegal for anyone except the state-endorsed Church of England officials to do so.

Bunyan was a metal worker by trade—an uneducated tinker. But his Spirit-filled preaching inspired people to passionately follow Jesus. His words were so powerful that throngs came to listen.[7] A day's notice would bring out a crowd of more than twelve hundred people for the next weekday morning. And that was long before the days of cell phones, texts, and social media.

When Bunyan was told one day that a warrant had been issued for his arrest and preaching that morning would most certainly get him in trouble with the law, he refused to shrink back and spoke anyway.

Sure enough, he was thrown in jail. He could have freed himself at any time by promising not to preach, but he refused. He told authorities that he would rather stay imprisoned until moss grew on his eyebrows than violate his faith and his principles. Bunyan stayed in jail for twelve years until the law he had broken was finally repealed.

Behind bars, Bunyan had much to fear. He faced horrible conditions—the lack of food, poor sanitation, overcrowding, the biting damp cold, and the jail fever and other diseases that often plagued and killed inmates. He knew that he might be executed. He feared for his wife and four children—especially for his special-needs blind child, of whom he was particularly fond. He sometimes feared that standing his ground wasn't the right decision. Promising not to preach would have alleviated all his suffering, and more importantly, all his family's suffering. Bunyan said he felt so troubled at times that he felt as though the flesh were being pulled from his bones.[8]

How did Bunyan combat these distressing fears? By embracing a greater, more powerful, calming fear—the fear of the Lord. He said, "[Fear] is a grace, that . . . will give you great boldness both with God and men."[9] This fear enabled him—as it had enabled Christian martyrs throughout history—to face "gaols [jails], and gibbets [gallows] . . . the sword and burning stake" with "the most mighty and invincible spirit that has been in the world!"[10]

Let that sink in for a moment.

Do you want to be a confident woman? One who possesses great calmness, great boldness, and the ability to face trouble with the most mighty and invincible spirit in the world? According to Bunyan, you *can* when you embrace the fear of the Lord!

"The fear of the LORD is Zion's treasure," declared the prophet Isaiah (33:6). Like the New York woman who sold an old white bowl at a garage sale, people who discard reverence as a beautiful aspect of fear fail to realize that they are scrapping a priceless treasure. Imagine her regret when she discovered that the bowl she sold for $3 was actually a one-thousand-year-old treasure from the Northern Song Dynasty worth $2.2 million.[11]

If we want to become confident women, we need to rethink our concept of fear. We need to wipe the dust off of this precious family heirloom and begin to value it for the treasure it is.

RETHINKING FEAR

Let's rethink fear. Fear is so much more than a negative emotion. Not only does this common perception fail to acknowledge that fear encompasses a healthy, positive fear of God, it also fails to acknowledge the way in which fear universally adds splashes of color to our lives.

Sometimes, fear is exciting and exhilarating. For many of us, the prospect of being scared out of our wits sounds like fun.

Just think of the crowds that line up to ride the sky-high roller coaster or the Drop of Doom at the local amusement park. Or the countless weekend warriors who participate in heart-pounding extreme sports like skydiving, zip-lining, hang gliding, rock climbing, heli-skiing, cave diving, or swimming with sharks.

Just think of all the people who flock to horror movies. Or the multitudes that visit haunted houses each Halloween. Or how much fun it is for a group of friends to jump out from behind the couch and holler "Surprise!" for a friend's birthday.

People can be drawn to fear-inducing experiences. Why? If fear were completely undesirable they'd avoid these experiences like the plague.

When the fear center of our brain is activated, our body is flooded with adrenaline, endorphins, and dopamine. "The natural high from the fight or flight response can feel great," explained Dr. Margee Kerr, a "scare specialist" who works as staff sociologist at ScareHouse, which heralds itself as "Pittsburgh's Scariest Haunted House."[12] "I've seen the process thousands of times from behind the walls in ScareHouse—someone screams and jumps and then immediately starts laughing and smiling. It's amazing to observe."[13]

People can actually enjoy the experience of feeling fear. Many relish the rush and thrill they feel when facing a risky, scary situation. Of course, to really enjoy it, they have to trust that even though they feel scared they will get through the experience safely.

When people watch scary movies their heartbeats increase, their palms sweat, their skin temperatures drop, their muscles tense, and their blood pressures spike. And interestingly, the more fear the moviegoer feels, the more that viewer claims to have enjoyed the horror movie. Researchers conclude that, oddly, "the most pleasant moments of a particular event may also be the most fearful."[14]

There's another positive dimension of fear that modern-day dictionaries don't address—the motivational aspect. Fear can be a powerful motivator. It can set you in motion to achieve more, experience more, and enjoy more.

Motivational speaker and author Patrick Sweeney says that fear is the fuel that drives ambition, courage, and success. He claims that embracing rather than rejecting fear is the key to confidence. "The way to a fulfilling life is not to avoid fear, but to recognize it, understand it, harness it, and unleash its power!"[15]

While Sweeney does not approach the topic of fear from a biblical perspective, I credit him for recognizing that there are some significant shortcomings in the way most of us think about fear and how we deal with this emotion.

God created humans with an intricate built-in fear system that originally included a healthy, positive fear of God. One of the most devastating effects of sin is that our fear network was damaged. Humanity lost its natural and wonderful fear of God. What's more, sin introduced a sweeping slate of dark, evil threats into our lives. As a result, people have almost lost sight of the fact that fear can be wonderful. Most people only experience fear as wonderful in brief, fleeting glimpses.

Fear is most certainly a crippling, debilitating emotion. But fear also has a remarkable, though widely neglected, positive side. It can be exciting and exhilarating. Thrilling. Motivating. Calming. Inspiring. Breathtaking.

Noah Webster knew this. John Bunyan knew this. William Brewster knew this. And so did the daughter whom he so audaciously named Fear.

I want to challenge you to reevaluate the way you think about fear. If you want to think about fear in a biblical way, you need to stop viewing it as a solely negative emotion. You need to reclaim those positive facets of fear that are largely absent from the modern-day definition.

A BROADER DEFINITION

At its root, fear is an emotion based on a comparison of relative strength. I compare myself to something and see that it is stronger than me. I feel fear when I am overwhelmed by an awareness that I don't measure up. The thing I'm facing has more capacity. More authority. More clout. More might.

When I am in a state of fear, I view that fear as extremely big and myself as extremely small. For example, I feel fear when I perceive that

the threat is bigger than my ability to stop it,
the problem is bigger than my ability to solve it,
the situation is bigger than my ability to deal with it,
the pain is bigger than my ability to bear it,
the loss is bigger than my ability to recover from it,
the expectation is bigger than my ability to live up to it,
the demand is bigger than my ability to fill it,
the force is bigger than my ability to match it, or
the power is bigger than my ability to control it.

If I perceive that the power of the "something" I am up against is a threat to my well-being, then the fear I feel is a negative feeling. If, on the other hand, I perceive that it is a benefit to my well-being, then the fear I feel is a positive feeling.

I'd like to propose a new definition for fear, one that's broad enough to encompass both a negative and a positive fear experience:

fear, *noun*

1. A strong or overwhelming sense that someone or something is greater than I am, and that it exerts a force beyond my control.

Fear is a strong or overwhelming sense. I identify it as a sense because it's more than just an emotion. Fear engages all the components of a person's fear network—emotional, intellectual, volitional, and physical.

It's *a strong or overwhelming sense.* In other words, fear has a significant and profound impact on me. It isn't like half-heartedly browsing through photos of the Grand Canyon in a glossy tourist brochure. It's more like standing on the edge of that gargantuan gorge in person and feeling stunned by its extraordinary dimensions.

Fear is a strong or overwhelming sense about *someone or something.* We can fear pretty much anything—a person, a place, an object, a situation, a deadline (says the girl who is trying not to panic about finishing this book on time), a circumstance, an event, an idea—anything.

Fear is a sense that someone or something *is greater than I am.* Again, it's a comparison of relative strength. When I am in a state of fear, I perceive that what I am facing is stronger and more powerful. What's more, *it exerts a force beyond my control.* Fear involves a feeling of powerlessness. Not only is this force much bigger than me, it has more authority. I can't direct it. I can't stop it. I am at its mercy. It will do what it wants. Fear involves feelings of uncertainty and ambiguity. Because I can't control the force, I can't be certain of the outcome.

This broad definition of fear embraces situations in which fear is experienced as a negative as well as situations in which fear is experienced as a positive.

Let's say you were going solo skydiving for the first time. You rig up, board the airplane, and nervously wait for it to reach an altitude of fourteen thousand feet. You've been instructed in skydiving basics. You know how to exit the aircraft, assume a free-fall body position, deploy and control your parachute, and land. You've jumped tandem with an instructor with a parachute system built for two. But this is your first time jumping alone.

The plane reaches the drop zone. The door opens. The noise is deafening. A tandem pair of jumpers are up first. The inductee gets on her knees and slides toward the opening. She screams in fear as she and her instructor disappear over the edge.

It's your turn.

Perched on the brink, you feel the adrenaline rush. You feel euphoric. Overwhelmed. Afraid. Your heart is pounding with fear, but you lean forward and jump anyway. Then you start to fall.

Fast.

Within a few seconds you're free-falling at about 120 miles per hour.

The wind buffets and exerts an upward pressure on your body while the force of gravity weighs and pulls you down. You are hurtling toward the ground as fast as a NASCAR driver speeding around the track at Myrtle Beach. It's scary, and yet at the same time inexplicably peaceful and serene. The sensory overload is indescribable.

The sky is vast. The earth is big. The pull of gravity is unstoppable. The wind is forcible. You feel puny and insignificant in comparison. At that moment, you are acutely aware that all these forces are greater than you are. They are beyond your control. You feel scared—but it's an exhilarating, thrilling type of fear.

The reason you're energized by this fear-inducing experience is because you trust your parachute to get you safely to the ground. But should your parachute and backup chute fail to deploy, your emotions would quickly flip from the positive to the negative side of fear. Panic and apprehension would replace the exhilaration.

Throwing yourself out of a perfectly good plane may not be your cup of tea. I only describe this scenario to show you that there's a razor-thin edge between a positive and a negative fear experience. The fear a skydiver feels in free-falling from a plane is only positive inasmuch as she can depend on her parachute to get her safely to the ground.

Hold on to that thought.

It's an important point that relates to what it means to have a healthy, positive fear of God. But before we dive in to that (pardon the pun), I want to flesh out the definition of fear for you just a bit more.

CATEGORIES OF FEAR

When I was a kid, one of my favorite games was sorting my mom's button bucket. She was a seamstress and never threw away a button. If a shirt or other piece of clothing wore out, she'd snip all the buttons off and toss them into the old ice-cream pail with all the other buttons. Then, she'd cut up the cloth and throw the squares into the rag bin out in my father's garage.

That button bucket was a source of endless fascination for me. I would dump all the buttons on the floor and sort them into categories. I might sort them by color, or by size, or by the material they were made of, or by whether they had shanks or not, or by the number of holes, or by whether they had metal or jewel accents. Sometimes I'd sort them into categories based on their use or how much I liked them. After I had categorized them, I'd put them back in the bucket, stir them up, dump them out again, and figure out a different way to categorize them. Weird, huh?

It must be my natural bent to group things together into categories because when I grew up, ideas became the "buttons" that I started to sort. And that's exactly what I've done with all the Bible verses about fear. I spread the thousands of verses out on the floor, so to speak, and tried to figure out how they relate to one another and the most natural way to group them together.

The way I see it, the biblical concept of fear can be divided into three basic categories: apprehensive fear, respectful fear, and reverent fear.

FEAR says, *This is bigger and more powerful than me and beyond my control . . .*

1. Apprehensive fear adds . . . *and it will likely harm me.*
2. Respectful fear adds . . . *and it is worthy of my regard.*
3. Reverent fear adds . . . *and it is worthy of my veneration.*

APPREHENSIVE FEAR

Apprehensive fear is the category that encompasses what most people think of when they hear the word *fear*—a scary, negative feeling. People experience this type of fear when they're afraid they will be hurt or negatively impacted by someone or something more powerful.

The Bible frequently mentions this type of fear. It depicts people as being afraid of God (Heb. 10:27) and of death (Heb. 2:15). Afraid of enemies (Ex. 14:10). Of family (Gen. 32:7). Of people in general (Deut. 3:22). Of criticism (Judg. 6:27). Of rejection (Ruth 3:11). Of hurting someone's feelings (1 Sam. 3:15). Of failure (1 Sam. 18:15). It shows them being afraid for their safety (1 Kings 19:3). Afraid of a political situation (2 Kings 10:4). Of threats (Neh. 6:19). Of getting sick (Deut. 28:60). Of suffering (Job 9:28). And of the future (Gen. 21:17).

It's clear that not much has changed. People in the Bible were scared of the same sorts of things that we are scared of today.

RESPECTFUL FEAR

Respectful fear is different than apprehensive fear. While apprehensive fear anticipates being harmed, respectful fear generally doesn't. It understands that the possibility of harm is mitigated by the exercise of proper regard.

Respectful fear involves being respectful or deferent toward someone or something that has greater power or position. I "fear" when I am careful to interact with the greater power in an appropriate way.

I would put extreme sports into this fear category. An ice climber fears the power of the glacier, for example. In other words, she has a healthy respect for its power. Before climbing, she carefully monitors ice conditions. She makes sure that her crampons are sharp, her axe and adze are strong, her ice screws are solid, and her belay and harness are securely fastened.

Or take a more mundane example, like power tools. I fear my circular saw. That doesn't mean I am frightened by it—on the contrary, I love it and use it all the time. Fearing my circular saw simply means that I'm careful to give it the respect it warrants.

The Bible implies that people ought to have a healthy respect (fear) for natural forces like lightning, thunder, rainstorms, raging oceans (Job 38), wild animals (Amos 3:8), and briers and thorns (Isa. 7:25). But the respectful fear that it encourages the most is toward those who occupy greater positions of authority.

Scripture instructs citizens to fear rulers (1 Peter 2:17), governing authorities and law enforcement (Rom. 13:3), and rules and regulations (1 Sam. 14:26). It instructs children to fear their parents (Lev. 19:3 KJV), servants to fear their masters (1 Peter 2:18 KJV), the young to fear the old (Lev. 19:32 KJV), congregants to fear their pastors (1 Thess. 5:12–13), and wives to fear their husbands (Eph. 5:33).[16]

Romans 13 tells us to pay to all what is owed to them: fear to whom fear is owed, honor to whom honor is owed (v. 7 KJV). We are supposed to respect those who hold positions of authority, for they are God's servants for our good (vv. 3–4).

Normally, we can anticipate benefit and not harm when we show proper respect. That's why English Bibles often use words like *respect* or *regard* in these contexts instead of the word *fear*.

REVERENT FEAR

The third category of fear is reverent fear. *Reverence* is a feeling or attitude of deep respect and veneration. It's holding someone or something in such high esteem that you elevate it to godlike status in your life.

The Bible teaches that although reverent fear ought to be reserved for God—he alone *is* God, after all—it is possible to have an idolatrous, reverent fear of other people or things. God demands an exclusive fear. He stipulates that we are to fear him and not other "gods."

The LORD made a covenant with them and commanded them, "You shall not fear other gods . . . but you shall fear the LORD . . . You shall not fear other gods, and you shall not forget the covenant that I have made with you. You shall not fear other gods, but you shall fear the LORD your God." (2 Kings 17:35–39)

The purpose of God's covenants, both old and new, is to make a way for humans to be restored into right relationship with him. A right relationship requires a proper view of who he is and who we are in relation to him. It requires an appropriate fear.

"What does the LORD your God require of you," summed up Moses, "but to fear the LORD your God, to walk in all his ways, to love him, to serve the LORD your God with all your heart and with all your soul" (Deut. 10:12).

The wise sage concurred. "When all has been heard, the conclusion of the matter is this: fear God and keep his commands, because this is for all humanity" (Eccl. 12:13 CSB). Or, as the English Standard Version puts it, fearing God "is the whole duty of man."

KNEE-KNOCKING FEAR

I loved thunderstorms as a girl, though we only got a handful of them each summer up in Western Canada where I lived.

Whenever I heard the skies begin to clap and rumble, I'd quickly grab a blanket and head outside. There was a narrow strip of dry concrete adjacent to the front door, where the overhang of the roof prevented the rain from hitting the steps. There, I nestled into the corner, tucked myself in, and settled down to watch the show.

Sometimes I'd stay in my cocoon for hours, fascinated by the barbed flashes of light that split open the sky. After each flash, I'd count—one one thousand, two one thousand, three one thousand—until the inevitable rumble of thunder interrupted my tally.

My mom would usually poke her head out the door to check on me and deliver a steaming mug of hot chocolate. If I was lucky, there'd be a big puffy white marshmallow bobbing in the froth.

The spectacle of lightning amazed me. To me, the jagged bolts were as entertaining as any New Year's Eve fireworks display. I was wowed.

I recall one big lightning storm that fired down hailstones the size of golf balls, some reaching the diameter of hardballs. I thought it was hilarious. I threw on a raincoat, ran into the garage to grab my dad's hard hat and a metal garbage can lid to act as a shield for protection, and sprinted around the yard collecting specimens.

I insisted that we store the biggest ones in the freezer, where they stayed for months so I could show them off to friends and brag of my exploits.

In retrospect, my attitude was rather callow. Have you ever heard that word, *callow*? It means immature or inexperienced. A callow is a young bald bird that's just hatched and hasn't grown any feathers yet.

I was naive. I didn't grasp the immense power of lightning. I didn't appreciate that it could be dangerous—even deadly.

Years later, while camping in the mountains, I found that out the hard way.

I was caught in the center of a horrific thunderstorm. The lightning and thunder were violent, incessant, and deafening. There was no counting between blinding flashes and earsplitting booms. Water streamed into my tent. The wind threatened to rip it from its pegs. I scrambled to collect my waterlogged gear and evacuate.

As I crawled out of the collapsing canvas, a massive bolt of lightning struck a tree nearby, sending fire and sparks erupting, bark exploding, and branches catapulting. My alarm escalated to panic. I threw myself to the ground. I was literally scared for my life.

That was the first time that lightning ever frightened me. I was overwhelmed by its power. It was so big and mighty. I was so small and powerless.

After that night, I wasn't a callow little bird anymore. I had grown some feathers. My attitude toward thunderstorms had matured from one of mere admiration to include fear, awe, and deep respect. From then on, I viewed lightning differently. And somehow, a greater appreciation for its power also increased my appreciation of its beauty.

Much like my childish, callow, laid-back attitude toward thunderstorms, I think that Christians in this culture often exhibit a callow attitude toward God. We love him—but don't revere him. We're entertained by him—but don't fall on our faces in awe. We call him friend—but don't tremble in his presence. We admire him—but don't fear him as our all-powerful, almighty Lord and King.

"If then I am [your] father, where is my honor?" the Lord asked in Malachi 1:6. "And if I am [your] master, where is my fear?"

In the Bible, knee-knocking fear is the natural response of those who encounter the glory of the presence of God. A few weeks after leading the Israelites out of slavery in Egypt, Moses prepared the newly liberated people to hear from God at Mount Sinai (Ex. 19). For two days they prepared themselves to ensure that they would be ceremonially clean. They also followed Moses' orders that no man or beast approach the mountain from which God would speak. If anyone even dared touch the mountain, he would die.

On the morning of the third day, a thick, dark cloud covered the top of Mount Sinai, blocking out the light of the sun. Brilliant white-gold flashes of lightning and loud claps of thunder reverberated from the midst of the black nebula. The people had seen plenty of thunderstorms before. But this was different. It was eerie.

Supernatural.

Otherworldly.

Though they couldn't see what was happening, they likely sensed the arrival of the hundreds of thousands of angelic beings that hovered invisibly overhead (Deut. 33:2). This supernatural influx undoubtedly sent shivers down their spines.

A deafening blast from a divine trumpet signaled that the Lord was about to descend and that it was time for Moses to bring the people to stand at the foot of the mountain. The people were already frightened by what was happening. As they moved closer, they positively shook with terror. Even Moses, who had previously encountered God's presence, felt terrified and trembled (Heb. 12:21).

Then, though it scarcely seemed possible, things got even scarier.

The Lord descended in a blazing inferno. Flames and acrid smoke exploded at the top of the mountain. The plumes billowed sky-high. The mountain quaked violently with seismic tremors. The blare of the unseeable trumpet escalated to deafening levels.

Moses called out to God, and God answered with a deep-pitched voice that boomed with greater power than the ear-piercing claps of thunder. The people were absolutely petrified. The sound reverberated through their bones as though they were standing directly in front of the subwoofer stack at an outdoor rock concert. The convulsing ground and blasting decibels shook them so violently that they could barely stand.

The overload on their senses was unbearable.

They were so visibly and physically assaulted with the holiness and majesty of God that they withdrew in terror from the foot of the mountain and begged Moses to make it all stop.

> Now when all the people saw the thunder and the flashes of lightning and the sound of the trumpet and the mountain smoking, the people were afraid and trembled, and they stood far off and said to Moses, "You speak to us, and we will listen; but do not let God speak to us, lest we die." Moses said to the people, "Do not fear, for God has come to test you, that the fear of him may be before you, that you may not sin." The people stood far off, while Moses drew near to the thick darkness where God was. (Ex. 20:18–21)

Moses informed the children of Israel that God let them experience the glory of his presence so that they would henceforth fear and obey him.

What happened at Mount Sinai was meant to strike the fear of God into their hearts. In other words, its purpose was to show them that God was much greater than they were—and also greater than all the gods of Egypt. He was a deity worthy of their veneration.

There are two kinds of fear mentioned in this passage: apprehensive fear and reverent fear. The former is the kind the people were to reject (Do *not* fear!) and the latter is the kind they were to embrace (*Do* fear!). Moses told them that they shouldn't *apprehensively* fear the Lord, for he was on their side and did not wish to harm them. On the other hand, they should *reverently* fear the Lord, for he deserved their awe, obedience, devotion, and worship.

In the weeks leading up to this encounter at Mount Sinai, the people of Israel had repeatedly questioned God. Moses hoped that an up-close glimpse of the glory of God would put an end to this sinful, callow attitude. He hoped that the knee-knocking display at Sinai would help his fellow Israelites learn to regard God with a lasting, reverent fear.

Their initial response was promising. They told Moses, "Behold, the LORD our God has shown us his glory and greatness . . . speak to us all that the LORD our God will speak to you, and we will hear and do it" (Deut. 5:24, 27).

Sadly, God knew that their newly awakened reverence would be short-lived. He lamented, "Oh that they had such a heart as this always, to fear me and to keep all my commandments, that it might go well with them and with their descendants forever!" (Deut. 5:29).

AN ESSENTIAL PARACHUTE

When the people of Israel saw God manifest himself in a cloud at the top of Mount Sinai, they feared for their lives. This fear was not unfounded. God is so glorious, so holy, so mighty, and so unspeakably awesome that sinful mortals would be totally obliterated if they physically came into his presence.

The New Testament explains that God dwells in unapproachable light. No one can see God and live (1 Tim. 6:15–16). His holiness and majesty are so great that we'd be totally consumed. "For our God is a consuming fire" (Heb. 12:29).

Even Moses wasn't allowed to gaze on the glory of God. Though he met and spoke with God in the tent of meeting "as a man speaks to his friend," their meetings were shrouded in a pillar of cloud (Ex. 33:11).

God is so overwhelmingly great that every person who ever caught a glimpse of him was overcome with fear.

Job exclaimed, "I am terrified at his presence . . . God has made my heart faint; the Almighty has terrified me" (Job 23:15–16). Ezekiel fell on his face when he saw a vision of the glory of the Lord (Ezek. 3:23). Isaiah came undone (Isa. 6:5 KJV). Overwhelmed and sapped of strength, Daniel fell face-first to the ground and barely managed to rise to his hands and knees, trembling (Dan. 10:9–10). Peter, James, and John were seized with fright when they saw Christ transfigured and heard the voice of God speak to them from a cloud (Mark 9:6). When the apostle John saw a vision of the risen Christ, he fell at his feet as though dead (Rev. 19:4).

When it comes to God, fear is the natural and appropriate response. People *ought* to tremble in his presence (Ps. 114:7).

Although it is appropriate to tremble in fear before God, the Bible insists that those of us who tremble in reverent fear should not tremble in apprehensive fear. If we truly fear God, we don't need to be afraid of God—or of anything else, for that matter. Reverent fear is the antidote to apprehensive fear and the foundation of strong confidence. *In the fear of the Lord one has strong confidence.*

Why? What's the reason for this do-fear/don't-fear paradox?

A few pages ago I asked you to hang on to this thought: The fear a skydiver feels in free-falling from a plane is only positive inasmuch as she can depend on her parachute to get her safely to the ground.

The parachute is essential, otherwise her encounter with gravity would most certainly end in disaster. It provides the safety equipment she needs to experience a thrilling, energizing, positive type of fear while skydiving. Similarly, the Lord has provided the "parachute" we need to safely enter into his presence. His gift of salvation enables us to experience a positive, enthralling type of fear when we draw near to God.

The writer of Hebrews contrasted the experience of the people who approached God at Mount Sinai with our experience approaching him now:

> For you have not come to what could be touched, to a blazing fire, to darkness, gloom, and storm, to the blast of a trumpet, and the sound of words. . . . The appearance was so terrifying that Moses said, I am trembling with fear. Instead, you have come to Mount Zion, to the city of the living God (the heavenly Jerusalem), to myriads of angels, a festive gathering, to the assembly of the firstborn whose names have been written in heaven, to a Judge, who is God of all, to the spirits of righteous people made perfect, and to Jesus, the mediator of a new covenant, and to the sprinkled blood, which says better things than the blood of Abel. (Heb. 12:18–19, 21–24 CSB)

The encounter at Mount Sinai demonstrated that it wasn't safe for sinful people to approach a holy God. To address this problem, priests offered daily sacrifices to make atonement for the people's sins. Once a year, on Yom Kippur (the Day of Atonement), the high priest entered the innermost sanctuary to meet with God and offer a sacrifice on the whole nation's behalf.

But it wasn't enough.

It didn't solve the problem.

The sacrificed animals didn't make the priests or anyone else holy enough to abide in the presence of God.

The writer of Hebrews explains that when Jesus died on the cross, he instituted a new and better way. Jesus did what the high priests of the old sacrificial system were unable to do. He completely took care of the problem of sin. Jesus secured eternal redemption for sinners (Heb. 9:12). Therefore, those who trust in Jesus can confidently approach God by Christ's blood (Heb. 10:19).

Moses brought the people of Israel to Mount Sinai to meet God, but Jesus brings us to a better "mountain"—the heavenly Mount Zion, the city of the living God.

What a contrast!

At Mount Sinai, the people had to stand at the foot of the mountain, at a safe distance from God. The mountain was shrouded in terrifying darkness, gloom, lightning, and thunder. The cacophony of the whirlwind, blaring trumpets, seismic tremors, blazing fire, and God's booming voice made the people shrink even farther back in apprehensive fear.

But now, Mount Sinai has given way to Mount Zion. The unapproachability of God has been eclipsed by the experience of full access to the presence of God through Jesus, the mediator of the new covenant.

The atmosphere at Mount Zion is completely different. It is jubilant. It is festive. The shroud of darkness is replaced by bright light and joyful, exuberant throngs of angels. It's a celebratory, festive atmosphere—a heavenly block party, so to speak. God is there. Jesus is there. Everyone who trusts in Jesus is there. They are "righteous people made perfect" (Heb. 12:23 CSB). God is still the great Judge, but because Christ's blood has covered our sin we are not consumed and are able to safely abide in God's presence.

FEAR-FILLED CONFIDENCE

You may be asking yourself what all this mountain imagery and theology about sin and salvation has to do with confidence. Let me assure you that it is highly relevant. Crucial, even.

The Bible teaches that it is impossible to have strong confidence apart from a relationship with Jesus Christ. It is because of Christ's sacrifice that we are able to confidently draw near to the throne of God. There, we "receive mercy and find grace to help [us] in [our] time of need" (Heb. 4:16). Thus, the confidence we have in approaching God gives us the confidence we need for every other circumstance. Regardless of how difficult the challenge we face, we can confidently say, "The Lord is my helper; I will not fear" (Heb. 13:6).

The writer of Hebrews warned us not to take this privilege for granted. He indicated that this great confidence in approaching God ought to be accompanied by an attitude of profound gratitude and reverent fear:

> See that you do not refuse him who is speaking. For if they did not escape when they refused him who warned them on earth, much less will we escape if we reject him who warns from heaven. . . . Therefore let us be grateful for receiving a kingdom that cannot be shaken, and thus let us offer to God acceptable worship, with reverence and awe [fear], for our God is a consuming fire. (Heb. 12:25, 28–29)

Reverent fear is the appropriate attitude we ought to have toward God. It was the attitude that God was looking for from the people who stood before him at Mount Sinai. How much more, argued the writer of Hebrews, should those of us who have been granted the right to confidently approach God's throne approach him with reverent fear? People who have the privilege of gathering with God on the heavenly mountain should fear him even more than those who trembled in his presence on the earthly mountain.

I hope you're starting to see the strong connection between confidence and fear. I hope that I've convinced you that the right kind of fear is a friend of strong confidence.

Job's friend rhetorically asked, "Is not your fear of God your confidence?" (Job 4:6).

It ought to be.

The kind of confidence that God wants us to have is a fear-filled confidence. The fear of the Lord is the companion of strong confidence and the antidote to all other fears.

If we want to be strong, confident women, we must learn how to be filled with the bold, beautiful, godly kind of fear that was cherished by the Puritans.

4

THE FEAR FACTOR

> There is a kind of fear that is not repulsive. It
> doesn't drive us away. It draws us in.
>
> —John Piper

Have you ever snapped a photo of a breathtaking sight—like a tropical beach, for example—and then afterward, when showing it to a friend, felt the need to add, "the picture doesn't do it justice"?

Because it doesn't.

A flat, two-dimensional pixel image is a poor substitute for being there in person. It's like handing your friend a program and expecting her to grasp what it was like for you to be at the Royal Albert Hall listening to the pulse-quickening "Nessun Dorma" performed by Pavarotti and the Royal Philharmonic Orchestra.

The cell phone photo of your tropical beach excursion doesn't capture the depth and breadth of the scenic kaleidoscope, the subtlety of the colors, the intricacy of the textures. It can't convey the full spectrum of sensations that overwhelmed your senses as you stood there: the sun's caress, the briny aroma, the salty tincture, the whispering fronds, the rhythmic anthem of crashing waves, the sandy foam playing hide-and-seek between your toes.

Most glaringly, a picture can't capture the sense of wonder that the awe-inspiring scene evoked in your spirit. Normally, it doesn't even come close.

Brad Lewis is an internationally renowned volcano and nature photographer whose work is often featured in *National Geographic* and on the Discovery Channel. Brad's volcanic art prints are displayed in exhibitions, museums, and corporate and private collections all around the world.

Brad is successful because his photos do far more justice to the scenery than most. His *LavArt* captures the raw beauty and power of volcanoes so brilliantly that the photos can awaken the type of wonder you'd feel if you were actually standing near a gushing fissure. Even so, I suspect that Brad would say that his photos don't quite do the trick.

You may remember watching coverage of the spectacular eruption of the Hawaiian Kilauea volcano a few years ago. News outlets provided footage of the angry crater spewing out geysers of blazing red magma, spectacular lava bombs, and sky-high plumes of volcanic ash. Fierce, unstoppable rivers of lava covered the landscape with molten rock and fire. Blazing volcanic waterfalls cascaded into the ocean, kicking up billowing, caustic clouds of laze (lava haze).

Most of us have watched fictional depictions of volcanoes, like Mount Doom in the classic movie trilogy The Lord of the Rings. Some of us have hiked up sharp volcanic rock to the edge of an inactive crater. But very few of us have experienced the power and beauty of an active volcano the way that Brad has.

He described the experience like this: "When I view hot lava gushing from the Earth, flowing down her flanks, and pouring into the ocean, I feel wonderfully small and insignificant, yet empowered by the eternal dynamics that make life possible on this planet."[1]

I find Brad's description fascinating. He feels "wonderfully small and insignificant." He feels exhilarated—"empowered." He feels awestruck in the presence of something that is greater than him—a force that is eternal, dynamic, creative, and somehow connected to life itself.

In a word, what Brad feels is fear. This is not an *apprehensive* type of fear. Though he acknowledges the danger, he doesn't expect to be harmed. This is a religious, *reverent* type of fear. It inspires him to venerate mother earth/nature. His feeling of smallness and insignificance in the face of the volcano's power is *wonderful*. What's more, it impacts him in a deep, profound way: it *empowers* him. What Brad described can only be characterized as a spiritual experience.

As Christians, we know that the awe-inducing fear that creation stirs in our hearts is actually a call to fear the Lord. The lesser fear points to the greater one. Creation speaks of *his* glory.

> The heavens declare the glory of God,
> > and the sky above proclaims his handiwork.
> Day to day pours out speech,
> > and night to night reveals knowledge.
> There is no speech, nor are there words,
> > whose voice is not heard.
> Their voice goes out through all the earth,
> > and their words to the end of the world. (Ps. 19:1–4)

Yet even if people haven't connected the dots and followed them to their ultimate source, they can still sense the numinous, mysterious power. They can feel the call and the pull of the supernatural. As Paul pointed out, "What can be known about God is evident among them, because God has shown it to them. For his invisible attributes, that is, his eternal power and divine nature, have been clearly seen since the creation of the world, being understood through what he has made" (Rom. 1:19–20 csb).

You've undoubtedly heard the saying "A picture paints a thousand words." It's true. Yet in the case of this mysterious pull, both the picture and the words fall short. We can't quite describe the wonderful feeling that is awakened when we are moved by a genuinely awe-inducing experience. The feeling is elusive, yet overwhelming and unmistakable. It whispers to us—often when we least expect—from the golden confetti of autumn leaves, the crescendo of music, or the laughter of a child.

It's an otherworldly pull. An inkling. An alluring fragrance that we can only whiff, a shadow whose shape we can't quite discern. It's a call that beckons us to draw near and lose ourselves in a fearful, wonderful feeling of smallness and insignificance in the presence of the almighty God.

MYSTERIOUS, FEARFUL, FASCINATING

Rudolf Otto was a German theologian and philosopher who lived in the early 1900s. He coined a Latin phrase to describe how humans feel in God's presence: *mysterium tremendum et fascinans.*

Mysterium means "mystery." God is a mystery to us because he is "wholly other." Because we are mortal and he is immortal, we can't fully understand his nature. He is unfathomable, far greater than human sensory or rational processes can grasp. Thus, when we come into contact with him, we regard him with blank wonder, awe, and stupor. We are gobsmacked—shocked, surprised, astounded, overwhelmed, dazed, discombobulated, baffled, confounded, stunned.

For example, when the people of Israel witnessed the power of God, they cried out, "We are undone, we are all undone" (Num. 17:12). Isaiah had a similar response. He also burst out, "Woe is me! for I am undone" (Isa. 6:5 KJV). *Mysterium* indicates that the supernatural blows our minds. It throws us off balance. It completely undoes us.

Tremendum is the second Latin word in Otto's phrase. It means "to shudder in reverent fear." We are filled with fear because we recognize that God's power is greater than our power. He exerts a force beyond our control. This fear is paired with reverence, for we recognize that he also outranks us. Not only is he greater in might, he is also greater in authority. He is dauntingly majestic. Thus, he deserves our veneration.

Otto called this the "creature feeling" or the feeling of "creature consciousness." "It is the emotion of a creature, submerged and overwhelmed by its own nothingness in contrast to that which is supreme above all creatures."[2]

The deep, inward shuddering that is indicated by the word *tremendum* is not fear in the ordinary sense of the word. Otto argued that man does not have the innate ability to fear God in the right way.

> The natural man is quite unable even to "shudder" (*grauen*) or feel horror in the real sense of the word. For "shuddering" is something more than "natural," ordinary fear. It implies that the mysterious is already beginning to loom before the mind, to touch the feelings.[3]

The ability to shudder in reverent fear isn't a natural human ability. Nor is this a natural human fear. This kind of fear can only be awakened by a personal encounter with God.

The final word in the Latin phrase is *fascinans*, which means fascinating. God's presence is daunting, but also compelling. It simultaneously repels and attracts. For those who love him, his power and majesty are experienced as uniquely beautiful and fascinating.

Yes, we are overwhelmed and awestruck in his presence. Yes, we fearfully tremble before him. At the same time, we find ourselves irresistibly drawn to him, attracted, and fascinated in ways we cannot fully explain.

His power, holiness, and justice frighten us, yet his love, grace, and mercy charm us. We can't understand him, nor can we control him, but somehow, this only serves to make us love and revere him more.

It's kind of like the relationship that Brad, the volcano photographer, has with volcanoes. He knows that the volcano is powerful and unpredictable. The hot, spewing molten lava could easily kill him. Nevertheless, he is fascinated by it and irresistibly drawn to its beauty. Rather than repelling him, the sheer, unbridled power mesmerizes and magnetically attracts him.

The complex mix of feelings we sense in the presence of our mysterious, fearful, and fascinating Lord reminds me of the part in the C. S. Lewis story *The Lion, the Witch and the Wardrobe* where Mr. and Mrs. Beaver are telling the children about Aslan, the lion who allegorically represents Christ.

"Is—is he a man?" asked Lucy.

"Aslan a man!" said Mr. Beaver sternly. "Certainly not. I tell you he is the King of the wood and the son of the great

Emperor-Beyond-the-Sea. Don't you know who is the King of Beasts? Aslan is a lion—*the* Lion, the great Lion."

"Ooh!" said Susan, "I'd thought he was a man. Is he—quite safe? I shall feel rather nervous about meeting a lion."

"That you will, dearie, and no mistake," said Mrs. Beaver; "if there's anyone who can appear before Aslan without their knees knocking, they're either braver than most or else just silly."

"Then he isn't safe?" said Lucy.

"Safe?" said Mr. Beaver; "don't you hear what Mrs. Beaver tells you? Who said anything about safe? 'Course he isn't safe. But he's good. He's the King, I tell you."

"I'm longing to see him," said Peter, "even if I do feel frightened when it comes to the point."[4]

C. S. Lewis beautifully captures the paradox. Aslan is not a man—he is a lion; *wholly other*. What's more, he is not just a common lion. He is the *great* Lion, the Lion above all lions, the King of Beasts. He is not tame. He cannot be controlled. The children's knees should rightly knock in Aslan's daunting presence. Yet, as Lucy's older brother Peter expressed, they could nevertheless look forward to meeting him. Though they trembled, it wasn't with a repulsive type of fear. It was trembling shot through with longing and eager expectation.

THAT'S FEAR SPEAKING

In the previous chapter, we learned that reverent fear says: "God is bigger and more powerful than me, beyond my control, and worthy of my veneration." In this chapter, we'll dig deeper into this multifaceted type of fear. You'll discover that this beautiful jewel is made up of five main facets: awe, obedience, devotion, worship, and trust.

AWE: HE IS GREAT BEYOND MY COMPREHENSION

The first facet of reverent fear is awe. The Bible commands us to "fear the LORD" and "stand in awe" of him (Ps. 33:8). So, what exactly is awe?

Most dictionaries define it as "the feeling of respect and amazement that you have when you are faced with something wonderful and often rather frightening."[5]

Often rather frightening. In other words, something that is delightful but might be a teeny bit scary too. Like an impressive Halloween front yard display, complete with spooky pumpkins, gauzy spiderwebs, eerie music, and a surprise, jump-out-at-you, menacing skeleton. "Ooh . . . that's awesome!" the trick-or-treaters exclaim.

At least this scenario contains an underlying hint of fear. Normally, fear doesn't even appear on stage. The way most people use the words *awe* and *awesome*, the connotation of fear is virtually absent. *Awesome* nowadays simply means wonderful. Fear and reverence are scarcely—if ever—involved.

The weather is awesome.

The TV show is awesome.

The outfit is awesome.

The pecan pie is awesome.

The cappuccino is awesome.

When we get to church and hear that God is awesome, the idea that comes to mind is that he is pleasant and enjoyable. He's delightful. Gratifying. Nice. We stand in awe of him the same way we stood in awe of the sunrise that made us feel all fuzzy and happy inside. Sadly, this view of awe falls markedly short of the biblical meaning.

A closely related word, whose meaning has also gone out of style, is the word *awful*. In the past, when someone described something as awful, they meant that it was awe-full. That is, it inspired the observer to be full of awe. For instance, John Bunyan recounted that the goodness and greatness of God stirred up an "awful reverence of his majesty" in his heart.

According to Noah Webster's 1828 dictionary, *awful* is that which "strikes with awe" and "fills with profound reverence."[6] When Bunyan described the reverence of God's majesty as awful, he meant that it stirred up a feeling of wondrous, trembling, holy fear.

Puritan Christians used the word *awful* in a positive way. To them, awful reverence was a holy and wondrous thing. But now, this concept is out of date. To modern minds, something awful is not wonderful. It's extremely disagreeable or objectionable. Why? Because nowadays, most people view fear of every kind as being bad, unpleasant, or ugly. But in the Bible's view, awe cannot be divorced from fear. *Awe* and *fear* are virtually the same thing.

We have stripped English words like *fear* and *awe* of their meaning. That's sad. Because when we lose the meaning, it makes it harder to grasp the concept. The words we have at our disposal simply aren't big enough to contain or communicate the idea.

During my research on the meaning of *awe*, I came across the website of Dr. Roy, a medical doctor who specializes in positive psychology and the science of happiness. Although Dr. Roy does not promote a Christian worldview, he perceptively notes that genuine awe is simultaneously saturated with both wonder and fear.

What is it to be in the grip of awe? How is it to feel the power of awe?

Awe is not merely a sense of wonder. Awe also does not mean a sense of fear. It is both, and still more powerful.

Awe is not a mere sense of wonder, because wonder does not frighten your being. Awe is not just fear because fear does not glue your gaze. It is a fusion of both, and yet more.

Awe means a heady brew of fear, admiration, delight, and surprise. In the presence of awe, you're afraid, and still, you stand to devour its thrill.

Awe is an intriguing and yet powerful experience. You feel it when you are fascinated by a spectacle, exceptional, and extraordinary.

As its grand scale holds you in a mesmerizing grip, you realize it's nothing like anything you have ever seen before.

Perhaps, we cannot explain awe as well as we can experience it. Awe does not share this quality with any other positive feeling. . . .

An experience of true awe engulfs you and re-frames your life in a way you never imagined before. It elevates your soul.[7]

Our modern concept of awe is contemptibly small. It is to the Bible's concept what a gentle ripple is to a towering tsunami. In Scripture's view, awe is the heightened emotional state of the creature in the presence of its almighty Creator, of the mortal in the presence of the immortal, of the natural in the presence of the supernatural, of the earthly in the presence of the divine. It is a heady brew characterized by fear, astonishment, and terror mingled with wonder, veneration, and reverence.

Awe is FEAR, ASTONISHMENT, and TERROR mingled with WONDER, VENERATION, and REVERENCE.

Rudolf Otto came up with the phrase *mysterium tremendum et fascinans* to describe this feeling that really can't be described.

Awe means we are dazzled—dumbstruck, stupefied, stunned—by the God who is wholly other. We feel afraid because we feel keenly aware of the extent of our own vulnerability. Yet at the same time we are entranced by his breathtaking glory. He is greater than our finite human minds can fathom.

- His power is matchless.
- His holiness is absolute.
- His excellence is unmatched.
- His justice is paramount.
- His sovereignty is unequaled.
- His beauty is unspeakable.
- His glory is transcendent.

Awe is a jaw-dropping, knee-knocking, pulse-quickening awareness of God's glory that shakes us to the core and radically reorients our perspective.

Awe of God engulfs us.

Reframes our lives in ways we never imagined.

Truly elevates our souls.

When was the last time you were in the grip of awe? Have you ever experienced the powerful mingling of wonder and fear in God's presence?

OBEDIENCE: HE IS WORTHY OF MY SUBMISSION

Awe is a deep, powerful emotion. But it doesn't stop there. Awe demands an active and appropriate response. If reverent fear is a diamond, awe is the all-important table facet—the top cut. The table facet functions as the diamond's window. It gathers light from above and directs it to the diamond's interior. The other facets reflect that light back up and out.

The second facet of reverent fear is obedience. I respond to an awareness of God's greatness with the appropriate action. He is God and I am not; therefore, I obey him. I humbly submit to his will. I joyfully acknowledge his absolute right to rule.

The Bible is clear that obedience is a crucial element of godly fear. "What does the LORD your God require of you, but to fear the LORD your God, to walk in all his ways?" (Deut. 10:12). Jesus affirmed that everyone who loves him obeys his teaching (John 14:23). He is the source of eternal salvation to all who obey (Heb. 5:9).

Reverent fear compels us to love the things that God loves and to hate the things that he hates. "To fear the LORD is to hate evil" (Prov. 8:13 CSB). Those who fear God embrace holiness and forsake sin (Ex. 20:20). They joyfully obey the Lord all the days of their lives (Deut. 6:2; 1 John 5:2). They aim to be holy in all their conduct—holy as he is holy (1 Peter 1:15–16).

Thus, if I truly fear God, I will turn away from

self-centeredness
materialism • envy • entitlement
conceit • condescension • disrespect • disdain
insulting • slandering • gossiping • bad-mouthing
lack of discipline • impulsiveness • headstrong attitude
callousness • cynicism • criticism • complaining
grudge holding • retaliation • backstabbing
self-indulgence • hypocrisy[8]

I will be loving, patient, and kind. I will not envy or boast or be arrogant or rude. I will not insist on my own way. I will not be irritable or resentful. I will never stop believing, never stop hoping, never give up (1 Cor. 13:4–7). I will not let any unwholesome talk come out of my mouth, but only speak what is helpful for building others up according to their needs (Eph. 4:29). I will not tolerate even a hint of sexual immorality in my life, nor will I tolerate any kind of impurity or greed, because these are improper for God's holy people (Eph. 5:3).

Ouch.

These verses reveal that I fall utterly short of God's standard. They inform me that I have a long, long way to go in developing a proper fear of God. But they also remind me of God's astonishing loving-kindness, mercy, and grace. Paul said, "For our sake he made him to be sin who knew no sin, so that in him we might become the righteousness of God" (2 Cor. 5:21).

I don't know about you, but this verse absolutely boggles my mind. It's *awesome*. It takes my breath away.

Just think. Jesus bore all our sins so we could be made holy before God. No condemnation now exists for those who believe in him (Rom. 8:1–2).

That means that although I miserably fail to meet God's standard, he does not condemn me for this. Through Jesus, I am holy in God's eyes. What's more, sin does not imprison me or rule over me, as it once did (Rom. 6:14). I am free to obey God. Indeed, I desire and delight to obey him in my inner being (Rom. 7:22).

The "she-is-holy" status conferred on me through Christ's death and resurrection inspires me to work at getting rid of the ugly sin in my life.

The *I have to* has become an *I want to*.

As C. S. Lewis so aptly put it:

Thus if you have really handed yourself over to Him, it must follow that you are trying to obey Him. But trying in a new way, a less worried way. Not doing these things in order to be saved, but because He has begun to save you already. Not hoping to get to Heaven as a reward for your actions, but inevitably wanting to act in a certain way because a first faint gleam of Heaven is already inside you.[9]

Paul tells us to work out our salvation with "fear and trembling" so that our characters increasingly match who God has proclaimed us to be (Phil. 2:12). This "fear and trembling" is not an apprehensive fear of judgment. In fact, it's the exact opposite.

Through Jesus we can be confident of our standing before God. Our obedience is motivated not by fear of punishment but by an awestruck, fearful awareness of the forgiveness that Christ has secured on our behalf. It is roused by gratitude, not guilt. It is not a *requisite* for forgiveness but an inevitable *result* of it. As the psalmist noted, "With you there is forgiveness, that you may be feared" (Ps. 130:4).

How are you doing in the obedience department? Do you delight to obey God? What does your level of obedience say about your need to grow in the fear of the Lord?

DEVOTION: HE IS WORTHY OF MY ALLEGIANCE

If you were to go on a tour of Japan, your guide would likely take you to see the bronze sculpture of a dog in the city of Shibuya, a ward of Tokyo. This statue is one of Japan's most famous meeting places. Many people take pictures with the bronze dog statue or lovingly adorn it with garlands of flowers. The nearby train station features the same dog on a massive, colorful mosaic wall. Even the manhole covers in the station are inscribed with bronze tributes to this famous canine.

The dog, whose name was Hachiko—Hachi for short—is honored in other locations in Japan as well. His fur is preserved and on permanent display at the National Science Museum of Japan. There's a bronze sculpture of Hachi at the University of Tokyo. There are also numerous sculptures and tributes in the city of Odate, his place of birth. What's more, you can purchase a trinket or memento of the dog in virtually every Japanese souvenir shop.

Why is Hachi so famous?

Hachi belonged to Dr. Ueno, a professor who taught at the Tokyo Imperial University in the early 1920s. Every day, Hachi would accompany Ueno to the Shibuya train station and then greet him again at the station when he returned from work. The pair continued this daily routine for several years. But then one day, the professor did not return. He suffered a stroke while lecturing and died without ever returning to the train station where Hachi waited.

Each day, Hachi showed up at the train station precisely when the train was due to wait for his beloved master. Hachi remained undeterred by other dogs or by people who tried to coax or chase him away. Day in and day out he arrived at the appointed time and watched expectantly as the passengers disembarked. When his master didn't show up, Hachi hung his tail in disappointment and sadly trotted home, only to return the next day to continue his vigil. After faithfully waiting for his master daily for nearly ten years, the loyal dog died. His cremated remains were buried at his owner's side. Hachi was finally reunited with the master he so adored.

Hachi's story became a sensation. His legendary loyalty became a national symbol in Japan, upheld as an example for everyone to emulate.

Devotion is the third facet of godly fear. Devotion means profound attachment and dedication. It involves love, loyalty, and heartfelt service.

The Bible repeatedly stresses that the fear of the Lord involves holding fast to him, clinging to him, and serving him with devotion (Deut. 10:12, 20; 13:4). "Cling to him and to serve him with all your heart and with all your soul" (Josh. 22:5).

The Hebrew word for *cling* is *dabaq*. It means "glue." The word is used in a literal sense of sticking to or adhering to something. But it is also used in the more abstract sense of sticking to someone in loyalty and devotion.

The fear of the Lord involves sincere and pure devotion (2 Cor. 11:3). Profound devotion. When we fear God, we *stick* to him as though glued. We faithfully hold fast to our faith (Heb. 10:23), to God's Word (Ps. 119:31), to his ways (Rom. 12:9), and to the hope of Christ's coming (Heb. 6:18).

The people of Japan could tell that Hachi was devoted to his master. If people were to observe your life, who or what would they say you were devoted to? Do your actions indicate that you stick to the Lord like glue?

WORSHIP: HE IS WORTHY OF MY PRAISE

From 2009 to 2011, Irish rock band U2 traveled around the world with their epic 360° Tour. Dubbed the Greatest Show on Earth, the tour made stops at stadiums in Europe, North America, South America, Africa, and Oceania.

The enormous 360-degree circular stage featured a 190-ton metal behemoth of four arches nicknamed "The Claw." The spider-like structure soared more than fifteen stories high, forming a sci-fi type cathedral, complete with a rotating platform, moving walkways, a monstrous speaker system, massive light rigs, and a huge central conical video display.[10]

Not only was it the most technologically innovative and expensive concert the world has ever seen, it was also the most well attended. Every single show of the tour sold out, many within minutes of tickets going on sale. All told, more than seven million concertgoers were wowed by the spectacular display.[11]

The 360° Rose Bowl concert in Pasadena, California, hosted a record-setting audience of almost one hundred thousand people.[12] The expansive crowd jumped, danced, cheered, and boisterously sang along with the famous band. When Bono broke into an a capella stanza of "Amazing Grace," the mass of people encircling the stage spontaneously raised their arms high in the air and swayed back and forth in a moment of worship-like solemnity. Then, when the band transitioned into U2's 1987 classic "Where the Streets Have No Name," the throng went absolutely wild: clapping, screaming, singing, and jumping in sync with the rhythm of the music.

Afterward, concertgoers raved about the experience. "It was legendary! Wonderful! Awesome! Stupefying!" One observer testified that there was something spiritual and otherworldly about the whole experience—like getting a glimpse of heaven.[13]

Some of you may not have heard of U2's renowned tour. It ended about a decade ago. The music stopped. The lights went out. And it's just a matter of time before it fades from memory and is upstaged by another "greatest show on earth."

As impressive as the show was, the awe of seeing Bono perform live in that venue cannot be compared to the awe we feel in God's presence. Not even close! The writer of Hebrews reminds us that if we believe in Jesus, we landed a ticket and are part of the crowd at a far more remarkable, dazzling show. Remember the passage from Hebrews 12?

> You have come to Mount Zion, to the city of the living God (the heavenly Jerusalem), to myriads of angels, a festive gathering, to the assembly of the firstborn whose names have been written in heaven, to a Judge, who is God of all, to the spirits of righteous people made perfect, and to Jesus, the mediator of a new covenant, and to the sprinkled blood, which says better things than the blood of Abel. (vv. 22–24 CSB)

There are myriads of angels in heaven. Elsewhere, we are told the heavenly hosts number countless thousands, plus thousands of thousands (Rev. 5:11). These descriptions indicate that the number of angels is immeasurable. The hosts of heaven cannot be counted (Jer. 33:22). Even if all seven million U2 360° Tour concertgoers were gathered together in the same venue, it would seem like a small, paltry audience compared to the attendance at this supernatural concert.

The Bible indicates that the host of angelic beings encircling God's throne praise him night and day. They continually extol his virtues. Did you notice how the writer of Hebrews described the scene? It's a *festive* gathering! They are exuberant! They can't contain themselves. Neither can the elders and the living creatures who, overcome with awe, constantly fall down and spontaneously worship God, exclaiming, "Amen. Hallelujah!" (Rev. 19:4).

In John's vision, a voice from near the throne exclaimed, "Praise our God, all you his servants, you who fear him, small and great" (Rev. 19:5). It's unclear who the voice belonged to; it may have been the archangel Michael, or perhaps it was one of the four living creatures. Nevertheless, what *is* clear in this exhortation is the unmistakable connection between the fear of God and worship. Whether small or great, those who fear him *praise* him!

Worship is the fourth facet of the fear of the Lord. *Worship* is a word that combines the prefix *wor-*, from the word *worth*, with the suffix *-ship*, which means "condition or shape." Therefore, worship has to do with the condition of being worthy. The best way to think about worship is that it acknowledges the "worth" of God. Our worship proclaims his worthship. In other words, it proclaims that he is *worthy* to receive honor and praise.

The myriads of angels in heaven boisterously sing, "Worthy is the Lamb who was slain, to receive power and wealth and wisdom and might and honor and glory and blessing!" (Rev. 5:12). Their praise extols God's worth.

It's the same with you and me. If we truly grasp God's worth—if we are truly awestruck by his fearsome glory—then we will naturally respond with thanksgiving and praise.

TRUST: HE IS WORTHY OF MY CONFIDENCE

The premise of this book is that the fear of the Lord creates strong confidence. The more we fear him, the less we fear other things, and the more confident we become.

By now you should know that confidence means trust. It's trust or faith in a person or thing. Fear and trust go hand in hand. When we fear God, we place our trust in him. We rely on his strength more than our own strength or the strength of other people or things. As David admonished, "You who fear the LORD, trust in the LORD!" (Ps. 115:11).

At the height of Christ's popularity, Jesus' disciples must have felt exceptionally confident about the future. They were sure that Jesus was the promised Messiah—the deliverer. In their opinion, this meant he would lead a political movement to get the nation of Israel out from under the rule of the Roman Empire.

Things looked promising. Extremely promising. The more miracles Jesus performed, the more followers he attracted. Crowds were increasing. Throngs of fans flocked to hear him. Jesus was a superstar! The movement was gaining momentum. One day, so many thousands came to see Jesus that they trampled over one another in their excitement to get up close to this up-and-coming celebrity (Luke 12:1). There were more people jostling for position than for the doorbuster specials at Best Buy on Black Friday.

The disciples were pumped. Euphoric! They were confident that Jesus was gaining the support they needed to successfully stage a revolution. If they were to overthrow the Romans, they would need public backing. A coup depended on it.

Jesus knew the disciples' confidence was misplaced. He knew the Jewish religious leaders were already secretly plotting against him. It wouldn't be long until Jesus was condemned to death and all his followers faced terrible persecution. The cheering fan club would disappear.

It was time for a reality check. Time to pop the fragile-confidence bubble that had his disciples floating on cloud nine. The guys were likely still backslapping and high-fiving over the size of the crowd when Jesus delivered this grim warning:

> Beware of men, for they will deliver you over to courts and flog you in their synagogues, and you will be dragged before governors and kings for my sake, to bear witness before them and the Gentiles. . . . Brother will deliver brother over to death, and the father his child, and children will rise against parents and have them put to death, and you will be hated by all for my name's sake. But the one who endures to the end will be saved. (Matt. 10:17–18, 21–22)

I suspect the disciples gave one another some quizzical looks at this point. They had no idea what Jesus was talking about. Why was he being such a negative Nelly? Naturally they'd encounter some resistance from the Romans. They expected no less. Yes, the going might get tough. But Jesus' popularity with the masses virtually guaranteed their success. There was little reason to fear.

Peter's confidence probably remained unshaken by Christ's dire prediction. He was likely thinking, *Bring it on. I'm ready to fight. I'm not afraid!* Peter could not have imagined that only months later, when the crowd turned, he would be so afraid that he would deny even knowing the man he believed was Israel's Messiah.

Jesus tenderly looked at his friends.

James, Son of Zebedee, would be the first disciple to die a martyr's death, beheaded for the crime of following Christ. The other James, Son of Alphaeus, would be sawed piece by piece into bloody chunks. Bartholomew would be shredded to ribbons with metal-toothed whips. Andrew would die bound to an X-shaped cross.

Matthew would be impaled with spears. Thomas would be assassinated. John would be exiled. Philip would endure the most tortuous death, dangled from his ankles like a carcass on iron hooks. Peter, too, would be martyred upside down, deeming himself unworthy to be crucified in the same upright position as his Lord.

Christ knew what was coming. He knew that his disciples would need strong confidence in order to stay brave to the end. He also knew that the only way they could gain the right kind of confidence was through the right kind of fear. They needed to put fear in its place. To have strong confidence, they needed to fear God more than they feared everything else.

Jesus continued his emotional plea:

> Nothing is covered up that will not be revealed, or hidden that will not be known. . . .
>
> I tell you, my friends, do not fear those who kill the body, and after that have nothing more that they can do. But I will warn you whom to fear: fear him who, after he has killed, has authority to cast into hell. Yes, I tell you, fear him! Are not five sparrows sold for two pennies? And not one of them is forgotten before God. Why, even the hairs of your head are all numbered. Fear not; you are of more value than many sparrows. (Luke 12:2, 4–7)

When Jesus said, "Nothing is covered up that will not be revealed, or hidden that will not be known," he was quoting a common saying that meant "the truth will triumph."[14] Knowing the severe persecution his friends would endure and the torturous deaths they would suffer no doubt added urgency to the message.

The truth will triumph . . . in the end.

I imagine the disciples stopped chattering and snapped

to attention when they noticed the serious look on Jesus' face. Obviously, both Matthew and Luke were impressed enough to remember and record his words. At the time, Christ's admonition may have just sounded like another paradox—a concept that on the surface is contradictory and doesn't seem to make much sense.

> Don't fear men.
> Don't fear persecution.
> Don't fear death.
> Fear God.
> Fear God's power.
> Fear God's authority.
> Fear not, he loves you dearly.
> Don't fear.
> *Do* fear!
> Don't fear!

Later, when facing persecution and death, it all made perfect sense. The disciples' fear of what man could do to them was eclipsed by a more powerful, more magnificent, calming fear. The great fear swallowed the lesser fear and infused them with courage and strength. Their fear of God was big, so their fear of man became small.

Fearing the Lord means making God—rather than my ability to secure a desired outcome—my confidence. With God as my confidence, the final outcome is guaranteed. Even if I have to endure the worst earthly case scenario, it is actually *not* the worst-case scenario. I can be confident that in the end, truth will triumph. The One who cherishes me so much that he numbers the hairs on my head will save me. I don't need to be afraid. Ultimately, I will be vindicated and will prevail in the only way that matters.

FEAR IS FOR FRIENDS

The whole point of the Bible is to teach people to reverently fear the Lord. Under the terms of the old covenant, God promised to bless those who approached him with reverent fear. In fact, his blessing was *contingent* on their fear. God said, "My covenant with him was one of life and peace, and I gave them to him. It was a covenant of fear, and he feared me. He stood in awe of my name" (Mal. 2:5).

The "him" in this verse is Levi—the Jewish ancestor at the root of the Levitical priesthood. Because Levi fulfilled his end of the bargain by fearing God, God fulfilled his end of the bargain by blessing him with life and peace.

The law and the sacrificial system were supposed to stir up the right kind of fear in people's hearts. Fear was the necessary ingredient. They needed to view God accurately and respond to him appropriately in order to be in a love relationship with him. The relationship was the end game. Ultimately, that's what the fear of the Lord is all about.

Some people under the old covenant did fear God the right way, but many feared him the wrong way. They weren't awed by God, nor did they exhibit loving obedience, devotion, worship, and trust. Instead of pursuing fear as the foundation of a relationship with him, they reduced it to a set of religious rules.

The Lord lamented, "This people draw near with their mouth and honor me with their lips, while their hearts are far from me, and their fear of me is a commandment taught by men" (Isa. 29:13).

God promised to initiate a new, everlasting covenant that would bring about a much, much better result. It, too, would be a covenant of fear. But instead of relying on human effort to fulfill the requirement, God would meet the requirement. He himself would put the right kind of fear into our hearts:

And they shall be my people, and I will be their God. I will give them one heart and one way, that they may fear me forever, for their own good and the good of their children after them. I will make with them an everlasting covenant, that I will not turn away from doing good to them. And I will put the fear of me in their hearts, that they may not turn from me. (Jer. 32:38–40)

How did God do this? Through Jesus, the One who epitomized what it meant to be filled with "the Spirit of knowledge and the fear of the LORD" (Isa. 11:2).

In case you are wondering, this Spirit is God's Holy Spirit. During Jesus' earthly tenure, this Spirit of the fear of the Lord rested on Jesus and inspired him to exhibit perfect awe, obedience, devotion, worship, and trust toward his heavenly Father. Jesus, "who in the days of his flesh, when he had offered up prayers and supplications . . . was heard in that he feared" (Heb. 5:7 KJV).

Even more astonishing than Christ's reverence toward his Father is the fact that the same Spirit that rested on Jesus now rests on us. All who come into God's covenant of grace have the fear of God, by the Holy Spirit, stamped on their hearts.

The beautiful jewel of godly fear is not something we must manufacture on our own. It is a gift that is wholly supernatural. And it becomes the prized possession of all who enter into a relationship with God through Jesus Christ.

If you believe in Jesus, the Spirit of the fear of the Lord is in your heart. This Spirit frees you from bondage to other fears. The right kind of fear frees you from the wrong kind of fear. Reverent fear calms apprehensive fear. "You did not receive the spirit of slavery to fall back into fear, but you have received the Spirit of adoption as sons, by whom we cry, 'Abba! Father!'" (Rom. 8:15).

The doctrine of fear isn't some pie-in-the-sky, boring, irrelevant theory. It offers you real, down-to-earth, practical hope and help in your battle against worry, doubt, and insecurity. The fantastic news is that God has already given you everything you need for victory. If you believe in Jesus, the Spirit of the fear of the Lord already lives within you.

Popular wisdom says the way to gain confidence is to have a bigger view of self. The Bible turns this strategy on its head. It teaches that what we need is not a bigger view of self but a bigger view of God. We don't need less fear—we need more! If we want to grow more confident, we need to get serious about the process of working out our salvation with fear and trembling. We must embrace awe, obedience, devotion, worship, and trust.

How do we get more of the right kind of fear and more of the right kind of confidence? The Bible provides the answer to this too. We ask. We seek. We knock.

And I tell you, ask, and it will be given to you; seek, and you will find; knock, and it will be opened to you. For everyone who asks receives, and the one who seeks finds, and to the one who knocks it will be opened. What father among you, if his son asks for a fish, will instead of a fish give him a serpent; or if he asks for an egg, will give him a scorpion? If you then, who are evil, know how to give good gifts to your children, how much more will the heavenly Father give the Holy Spirit to those who ask him! (Luke 11:9–13)

When we ask, seek, and knock, our heavenly Father will surely answer. He will fill and empower us with the Spirit of fear who brings us strong confidence.

5

FOUNDATION OF CONFIDENCE

> Oh, how great peace and quietness would
> he possess who should cut off all vain anxiety
> and place all his confidence in God.
>
> —Thomas à Kempis

If you're looking to build your confidence, you'll find no shortage of advice. The internet offers books, workshops, and training courses by all sorts of self-help experts, all who promise to help you overcome your fears. And ever since Sheryl Sandberg rocked the corporate world with her claim that fear and self-doubt are at the heart of what is holding women back from success, a new kind of self-help expert has started to dominate the field: the feminist confidence guru.

Confidence instruction is the latest feminist fad, and women are lapping it up. One popular purveyor is Kasia Urbaniak—an ex-dominatrix turned female empowerment coach. Based out of New

York, Kasia is the founder and headmistress of The Academy, "a secret school that teaches women to fully embody their confidence and power."[1]

Kasia promises students they can break out of years of good-girl conditioning, step into their power, and gain the internal confidence they've always lacked.[2] She credits her years as a dominatrix—a woman who is paid to play the dominant role in BDSM sexual encounters—for teaching her about confidence and power dynamics.[3] Kasia claims that suppressed female desire giving itself permission to be heard is the key to a woman's confidence. Her confidence formula is that women need to drop the "good girl" persona and become more "bad girl" in demanding what they want.[4] Women need to connect with their deep desires "with total self-celebration and no self-attack."[5]

Another guru is Mama Gena, who runs The School of Womanly Arts. Her Five-Day Self-Love Mini-Course promises to awaken "your most confident, radiant self."[6] Her solution to women's lack of confidence is that we need to tap into the feminine truth and power deep within and learn to trust ourselves in a bold new way.

If attending confidence seminars or confidence college courses aren't enough, you can get individualized instruction from a personal confidence coach. Confidence coaches have popped up on the internet faster than stuffed critters in a game of Whac-A-Mole.

These coaches promise to help you build your confidence. For only ninety-nine dollars a session (on the affordable end), a confidence expert will work with you to overcome all your personal fears and insecurities. She'll have you living a transformed and more self-expressed life before you can even say, "Hey, check me out! I'm a self-confident woman!"

The promises are many.

- Discover your authentic self.
- Fall in love with yourself.
- Celebrate yourself.
- Trust yourself.
- Overcome your fears and limitations.
- Be more. Do more. Have more.
- Live an AWESOME and fulfilling life! (*AWESOME* with all caps, of course.)

What's more, after you've pumped some air into your own tires, you'll be able to put your newfound expertise to good use by helping others. For as low as $139.99 you, too, can become a certified confidence coach.

The whole confidence industry would be laughable if it wasn't so lamentable. It is profoundly sad that so many women are plagued with crippling doubts, insecurities, and fears. But it is equally sad that the cure the confidence gurus promote merely perpetuates the problem. Women have swallowed the feminist self-confidence prescription for decades. Now, we are being promised that our confidence problems will be resolved by upping the dosage of this familiar blue pill.

That's like the quack telling a patient who suffers from the side effects of snake oil that she just needs to double her intake.

The overarching message of the confidence industry is that women need to learn to love and trust themselves more. Of course, when you think about it, this solution isn't really a solution. For if a woman fails to make significant progress against self-doubt, that just gives her more reason for self-doubt. Her lack of confidence is simply another sign of her inadequacy.

This generation's women have been mentored in the art of self-affirmation. We've been raised to embrace the just-love-and-trust-yourself-more mantra. Yet oddly, this has merely resulted in a false bravado. We may appear confident—assertive, assured, commanding, or even brash, cheeky, and aggressive. However, under the fragile veneer, it's just an act. Our confidence is fleeting. Most often it's phony, a well-crafted performance intended to mask the underlying fears that gnaw at our souls.

If you lack confidence, telling yourself to have more confidence will not work. If you lack self-esteem, telling yourself to have more self-esteem won't work. If you are filled with self-loathing, telling yourself to love yourself more won't work. Giving yourself a pep talk is not a lasting solution. What you actually need is to stop relying on yourself, or on other people or things, for confidence. God beckons you to turn to an infinitely greater, more powerful, and more trustworthy source.

RED PILL VS. BLUE PILL

Scripture insists that for a believer, confidence flows from an entirely different source than the type of confidence the world promotes. Christian confidence is having faith in God's character, God's power, and God's promises rather than in human capacity or achievement. It depends on what God has done and can do rather than on what we have done or can do.

Confidence is about trust. As such, it is virtually indivisible from faith, belief, hope, and assurance. Indeed, confidence is the very essence of faith. "Faith *is* confidence," declared the writer of Hebrews. "Confidence in what we hope for and assurance about what we do not see" (Heb. 11:1 NIV, emphasis added). Faith means putting our trust in God through Jesus Christ and believing his promises, even though those promises are not yet fully realized and even though we do not yet see him face-to-face.

Christian confidence is being convinced that God is who he says he is and that he will do what he says he will do. It is having rock-solid faith in the Lord. *He* is the object of our trust. *He* is our confidence. Therefore, the foundation for strong confidence is an accurate view of God.

It's important for us to remember that our battle for confidence isn't merely about our apprehension of being judged or disliked. Our confidence battle takes place on a much larger, cosmic stage. It is a subset of the battle between truth and error, right and wrong, good and evil.

There are two powerful forces vying for our trust: God and Satan.

God wants our trust. He deserves our trust. He is worthy of our trust. But God's archenemy, Satan, wants to trick us into trusting everything and anything but God. Satan is the ultimate con artist. The reason sin exists in our world is because he pulled the wool over humanity's eyes and won the confidence game. His strategy has not changed. He convinced Eve to doubt God and to put her faith in all the wrong things. And he wants us to fall into the same trap.

Satan peddles doubt so he can peddle confidence. He is a fear-monger who promotes uncertainty, insecurity, anxiety, and despair. Then, he promotes fragile, foolish confidence to address this wound of the soul.

He's like the swindler who sells you a cheap bike with leaky tires and then sends a business partner to your door the next day to sell you a pump. At the same time, this master conniver engages in a relentless smear campaign of fake news and false advertising to undermine your trust in the competitor's product.

One of the most famous parts of the sci-fi movie *The Matrix* is the iconic red-pill-or-blue-pill scene. If the hero takes the red pill, he will escape the fake, computer-generated world of the Matrix. He will be freed from the deceptive fantasy and be able to see reality for what it is. If he takes the blue pill, he will remain under the spell of the computer's mind-controlling delusion.

The status of your confidence depends on which pill you swallow. If you take Satan's blue pill, your confidence will be based on a matrix of deception. The Bible is adamant that only when we rely on God will we have strong, smart confidence. Trusting in anything else puts us in a fantasy world where our security is nothing more than a fragile illusion.

A DOSE OF REALITY

The Bible contains numerous examples of people who learned to reject the deceptive confidence pill. Moses is the protagonist of one of the most dramatic stories. He once was a swallow-the-blue-pill kind of guy. That's not to say he was a regular kind of guy. He had far more going for him than most. Although he was born to a Hebrew slave, he was adopted by an Egyptian princess. Therefore, he was raised in the palace among the elite as Pharaoh's grandson. Moses grew up steeped in riches, power, and privilege. The Bible tells us that "Moses was instructed in all the wisdom of the Egyptians, and he was mighty in his words and deeds" (Acts 7:22).

Moses was a respected and accomplished military commander. He was smart. Capable. And probably handsome too. He had confidence. Swag. Theologians suggest that his royal mother proposed to make him coregent and successor to the crown or to assume another powerful position in Egypt. But there was a problem.

Over the years, as Moses observed the Egyptians' brutal treatment of the enslaved Hebrews, he grew increasingly sympathetic to their plight. Yes, he had been raised Egyptian, but Hebrew blood flowed through his veins. Feisty Moses became a vocal advocate of the slaves. This created conflict in the palace and especially with his mom. So much so that it finally came to a head. Moses "refused to be called the son of Pharaoh's daughter" (Heb. 11:24).

Moses wanted to leverage his power and position to improve the plight of the slaves. Perhaps he could convince the Egyptians to treat them better. Or perhaps he could rally the Hebrews and lead a revolt. Moses rashly thought he could deliver his people—God's people—in his own strength and at his own time. But then something happened to totally shatter his confidence.

One day, when Moses had grown up, he went out to his people and looked on their burdens, and he saw an Egyptian beating a Hebrew, one of his people. He looked this way and that, and seeing no one, he struck down the Egyptian and hid him in the sand. When he went out the next day, behold, two Hebrews were struggling together. And he said to the man in the wrong, "Why do you strike your companion?" He answered, "Who made you a prince and a judge over us? Do you mean to kill me as you killed the Egyptian?" Then Moses was afraid, and thought, "Surely the thing is known." When Pharaoh heard of it, he sought to kill Moses. But Moses fled from Pharaoh and stayed in the land of Midian. (Ex. 2:11–15)

Moses was stunned. The Hebrews didn't view him as a potential savior; they viewed him with contempt. Moses stuck his neck out for them—risked everything—yet they rejected him. What's more, the crime put him past the point of return with his adopted Egyptian family. As expected, Pharaoh, his grandfather, issued an imperial decree to put him to death. Moses couldn't return to the palace. He was homeless. The Hebrews didn't want him. The Egyptians were out to kill him. In an instant, all his riches, privilege, power, position—everything in which he placed his identity and trust— were gone.

The Bible picks up the story forty years later. Moses' life has turned out far different than he expected. He's an alligator-skinned eighty-year-old. And all he's done for the past 14,600 days (plus or minus a few) is tend sheep. Moses is a shell of his former self. And no wonder. Shepherds were the lowest of the low. The young, confident, in-it-to-win-it Moses was but a distant, faded memory. He'd become a wrinkled old man, fearful, insecure, and riddled with self-doubt.

That was the state of affairs when God spoke to Moses from the burning bush, commanding him to return to Egypt to lead the Hebrews out of slavery. Moses was reluctant to obey. He said, "Who am I that I should go to Pharaoh and bring the children of Israel out of Egypt?" (Ex. 3:11). In fact, he came up with multiple reasons why he wasn't the right person for the job.

What's interesting about the narrative is that God didn't engage Moses in a rah-rah, shot-in-the-arm, "I-know-you-can-do-it-Moses" coaching session. He didn't list all of Moses' past credentials and accomplishments. Quite the opposite, in fact. He rebuked Moses for hinging his confidence on his own ability.

Moses lacked confidence because he was focused on his own inadequacy. God wanted to reorient his perspective. He wanted Moses to focus on God's ability rather than his own inability. Whenever Moses brought up an objection based on a personal deficiency or fear, God countered it with the truth about his own nature and character. It was this truth that would build Moses' confidence. Moses didn't need a new or bigger view of self. He needed a new and bigger view of God.

First, Moses objected that the Israelites would question whether he had truly encountered God. In response to this objection, God revealed more of himself to Moses. He told him his holy, memorial name: Yahweh, the great I Am. He is God. He is everything he says he is.

Moses could trust that God "is." He could trust God's person.

Second, Moses objected that the Egyptians would not accept him as God's spokesman. "But behold, they will not believe me or listen to my voice, for they will say, 'The LORD did not appear to you'" (Ex. 4:1). In reply to this, God gave Moses a sign: Moses' staff turned to a snake and back to a staff. His hand became leprous and was then healed.

Moses could trust that God is able. He could trust God's power.

Next, Moses objected that he wasn't good with words. He was "slow of speech and tongue" (Ex. 4:10). Some theologians suggest that Moses had a speech impediment. Perhaps he had a stutter. According to one Jewish tradition, Moses had difficulty pronouncing the labials *b, v, m, ph, p.*[7] Other academics suggest that Moses was worried about communicating in the Egyptian language, which he hadn't done for decades. Still others speculate that he was intimidated by public speaking.

It isn't entirely clear what Moses meant when he objected that he was slow of speech and tongue. But it is obvious that Moses lacked the confidence he needed to get the job done. He simply did not think he could do it.

How did God respond to the bellyaching of this desert shepherd?

He reminded Moses that God was the one who created Moses' mouth. Thus, Moses' mouth belonged to God: "Then the LORD said to [Moses], 'Who has made man's mouth? . . . Is it not I, the LORD? Now therefore go, and I will be with your mouth and teach you what you shall speak'" (Ex. 4:11–12).

Again, the Lord didn't give Moses a pep talk. He didn't fix Moses' speech problem. Nor did he indicate that Moses would eventually get better at public speaking. Instead, he corrected Moses' faulty perspective. This wasn't about Moses; it was about the Lord! Moses' competence had nothing to do with it. He didn't have to rely on his own ability. Nor did he have to worry about his inability. God would be with him and help him. All Moses had to do was put his confidence in God.

Moses could trust that God would help. He could trust God's provision.

Still, Moses begged God to send someone else. God was not pleased with this lack of trust. Nevertheless, he promised that Aaron, Moses' elder brother, would help, and that God would teach both of them what to say and do (Ex. 4:15).

Adding Aaron into the equation didn't take God by surprise. It was his plan all along. Aaron became Israel's first high priest. He bore "the judgment of the people of Israel on his heart before the LORD regularly" (Ex. 28:30). According to the New Testament, Aaron prefigured the Messiah. Just as God appointed Aaron to be the first high priest of the old covenant, so he appointed Jesus to be the first (and only) high priest of the new covenant. When Jesus died on the cross for our sins, he bore our judgment on his heart before God once for all time. That's why we can confidently draw near to God (Heb. 7).

Moses and Aaron were God's chosen tag team in an eternal story. They couldn't have known the part they would play in his overall plan. They were simply focused on their immediate assignment—leading the Hebrews out of slavery to the promised land. They didn't understand that this deliverance foreshadowed God's plan for an even greater deliverance.

Moses could trust that God would deliver. He could trust God's plan.

Moses was eighty years old when God asked Moses to be his mouthpiece. At the time, Moses was absolutely terrified by the thought. He felt insecure, impaired, and incompetent.

He must have learned a thing or two along the way, because forty years later, we see that Moses had radically changed. The man who had been terrified to open his mouth stood with quiet confidence to address the entire nation as they stood on the cusp of entering the promised land.

The Bible tells us that Moses recited the words of a long song from beginning to end. At the end of the song, Moses did not stop. His speech continued. One by one he blessed the tribes. His oratory fills two entire chapters of Deuteronomy.

The book concludes with this assessment: "No prophet has arisen again in Israel like Moses, whom the LORD knew face to face. He was unparalleled for all the signs and wonders the LORD sent him to do against the land of Egypt—to Pharaoh, to all his officials, and to all his land—and for all the mighty acts of power and terrifying deeds that Moses performed in the sight of all Israel" (Deut. 34:10–12 CSB).

The young, feisty Moses, swagged-out and sure of his own ability, was not the Moses that God wanted for the big assignment. God knew that Moses was addicted to the blue self-confidence pill. He was placing his trust in his own strength. His confidence was a fragile illusion. After all the props were kicked out, Moses was ready for the red pill. Fearful, insecure Moses was ready to learn that strong confidence is really only found in God.

God changed Moses from a washed-up, insecure coward into a mighty, eloquent leader. He transformed Moses' inability to ability, his weakness to power, his insecurity to strong confidence. Moses overcame his propensity to reach for the blue pill and learned to habitually reach for the red. What God did for Moses he can do for you.

Whether you are more like the brash, swaggering Moses or the fearful, inadequate Moses, you can also learn to say no to the wrong kind of confidence and yes to the right kind of confidence. You can learn to put your trust in God. Remember:

- GOD IS. You can trust his person.
- GOD IS ABLE. You can trust his power.
- GOD WILL HELP. You can trust his provision.
- GOD WILL DELIVER. You can trust his plan.

God is in the confidence-building business. And unlike the shallow stuff pushed by modern-day confidence gurus, his brand of confidence has the power to dramatically change your life.

A CONFIDENCE LESSON

So how does confidence in God help you when you're feeling insecure about the presentation you have to give? Or stressed about having too much to do? Or anxious that you can't pay the bills? Or dismayed about relational conflict? Or scared about a medical diagnosis? Or panicked by some terrible news? How can you respond with faith and not fear when life hits you with problems and the future seems so uncertain?

Many of us go through life in a constant state of low-grade fear. Like a boat seesawing through choppy waters, our spirits are tossed about by stress, worries, doubts, and anxieties.

For many of us there are choices we can make to help quiet the chaos swirling around us. We can volitionally take clutter out of the present moment. But what about those times when life broadsides us with a huge wave that we can't do anything about? Like sickness, death, a wayward child, an unfaithful husband, or a fractured relationship? How can we have peace and confidence in those circumstances?

I've had huge waves hit my boat over the years. Like when my youngest son lost his hearing at age two. Or when I miscarried twins. Or the time we almost lost another son to staph infection. Or the time my husband's business was in crisis. Or the legal drama. Or the car accident. I've been rocked by family conflicts, church conflicts, betrayals, and disappointments. Many, many storms have crashed into my boat.

I know that you have had significant storms in your life too. We can all relate to Job, who, reeling from being hit, lamented, "I cannot relax or be calm; I have no rest, for turmoil has come" (Job 3:26 CSB). Or to the disciples in the boat on that stormy night, who in fear and panic screamed at Jesus with the question, "Don't you care that we're drowning?!"

The disciples learned an important lesson that night. They learned that apprehensive fear is quelled by reverent fear. To face the storm with confidence, they had to gain a greater understanding of who was riding in their boat.

Here's how Mark described what happened:

> On that day, when evening had come, he said to them, "Let us go across to the other side." And leaving the crowd, they took him with them in the boat, just as he was. And other boats were with him. And a great windstorm arose, and the waves were breaking into the boat, so that the boat was already filling. But he was in the stern, asleep on the cushion. And they woke him and said to him, "Teacher, do you not care that we are perishing?" And he awoke and rebuked the wind and said to the sea, "Peace! Be still!" And the wind ceased, and there was a great calm. He said to them, "Why are you so afraid? Have you still no faith?" And they were filled with great fear and said to one another, "Who then is this, that even the wind and the sea obey him?" (Mark 4:35–41)

The Sea of Galilee is subject to being hit by sudden, unexpected storms. In this account, the disciples panicked when a particularly violent squall hit. They were afraid that the tempest was going to overwhelm them.

But Jesus rebuked them for their response. According to Jesus, with him in their boat, they ought to have experienced peace—and not panic—in the middle of the storm.

Why did the disciples experience panic instead of peace that stormy night at sea? The thoughts and attitudes that killed their confidence are the same ones that produce panic in our spirits when we face frightening situations. Ultimately, their fear stemmed from their inadequate view of Christ and a lack of faith in him. To gain confidence they needed a bigger and more accurate view of God. Let's take a closer look at the three confidence killers they let take over and how we can avoid going down the same path.

MISPLACED FEAR: "GOD IS NOT BIG ENOUGH."

The disciples experienced two types of fear. One type was misplaced, and the other was not. The first type of fear was an apprehensive fear. They were afraid that the storm was going to overwhelm them and that they were going to drown. It must have been quite the storm to frighten them! They were seasoned fishermen, after all, and were accustomed to conditions on the sea. But when this particular storm hit, even those seasoned mariners panicked.

What's interesting is what we read further on in the passage. The squall hit, and the disciples were afraid, but then Jesus calmed the storm, and the sea became perfectly still. "The wind ceased, and there was a great calm." And what was their response? They were terrified!

The disciples were more afraid of the power of Christ than they were of the power of the storm. Verse 41 says they were filled with "great fear." The Greek reads *megas phobos.*

Megafear!

Mega, as you know, means "great." The metric system uses it as a prefix to denote a factor of ten to the sixth power, or one million times more. For example, a pixel is one tiny colored dot of a digital image—a megapixel is one million dots. A watt is one standard unit of power—a megawatt is one million watts. A byte is one unit of data—a megabyte is one million units. You get the idea.

This passage uses the word *mega* a lot: There was a megawindstorm. Jesus produced a megacalm. The disciples felt a megafear.

The disciples were afraid of the storm. But what they felt when Jesus calmed the storm was a million times more intense: They felt megafear. Reverential fear. Fear of God.

Remember that at its root, fear is an emotion that is based on a comparison of relative strength. *Fear is a strong or overwhelming sense that someone or something is greater than I am, and that it exerts a force beyond my control.*

When I experience apprehensive fear, I feel afraid because I recognize that what I am facing could hurt me and expect that it likely will. Whether the storm has to do with a fractured relationship, my marriage, my children, my family, my friends, or whether it has to do with a loved one's health, my finances, pressures at work, death, grief, or loss, I realize that I am not big enough to handle whatever it is.

I don't have the resources.
I don't have the time.
I don't have the ability.
I don't have the capacity.
I don't have the confidence.

I've tried and tried, but I can't stop the boat from pitching. This situation is beyond my control, and it's overwhelming me!

Apprehensive fear produces panic and anxiety. But reverential fear is quite different. Reverential fear is a positive emotion. It produces awe, worship, and righteousness. It brings peace. And it builds confidence.

Jesus wanted the disciples to recognize that he was bigger and more powerful than any circumstance they might face. He was a million times greater than the storm that was causing their fear.

You see, the disciples' fear was misplaced. They feared their circumstances more than they feared Christ. They saw their circumstances as bigger than him.

Their core belief was *God is not big enough.*

Have you ever thought that? Have you ever looked at your circumstances and thought, *This one is too big . . . even for God!*

He can't bring love back into *this* marriage.

He can't change *that* person's heart.

He can't bring back *that* wayward child.

He can't cure *this* illness.

He can't restore unity to *this* church.

He can't resolve *this* crisis.

He's just not big enough!

Maybe you wouldn't say it in so many words. But your anxiety and lack of peace indicate that's what you genuinely believe.

The disciples in the boat on that stormy night thought, *Jesus can't do anything about this storm. These circumstances are out of his control.* But then Jesus got up and showed them that even the wildest, most ferocious storm is not out of his control. And when they saw his power and glory, they were terrified, fell on their faces, and asked one another, "Who is this man in our boat? We had no idea he had this much power!" The disciples didn't get it. They respected Jesus as a great teacher, but to grow in confidence, they also needed to revere him as God.

When our fear is misplaced, our primary concern is being at peace with our circumstances. We want the storm to be calm. But when we see Christ for who he is—the almighty God and King of Glory—our primary concern is being at peace with *him*.

Being in the right circumstance may not bring peace. But Scripture teaches that being right with God will give you peace and quiet confidence: "The result of righteousness will be peace; the effect of righteousness will be quiet confidence forever" (Isa. 32:17 CSB).

True peace is not dependent on circumstances but on a person. Jesus is the Prince of Peace. He is our confidence. He orders chaos. He reconciles relationships between God and man and between man and man. He is the One who gives rest, peace, and quiet confidence forever.

Jesus said, "Peace I leave with you. My peace I give to you. I do not give to you as the world gives. Don't let your heart be troubled or fearful" (John 14:27 CSB). The kind of confidence that Jesus gives is different from the kind of confidence the world gives. It's a rock-solid, strong confidence that will see us through any storm.

MISPLACED TRUST: "GOD IS NOT INTERESTED ENOUGH."

The disciples were in great danger. The waves were breaking over their boat so severely that it was nearly swamped. They were undoubtedly doing some pretty serious bailing. I imagine they were scooping water out of the boat just as fast as they could—with buckets, boots, bowls—anything that could scoop.

At first they trusted their own capacity to keep the boat from going under. They were fishermen, after all. They knew how to respond to storms at sea. I suspect that Peter took charge and shouted out orders: "All hands on deck! Mark, over here! Matthew, over there! Bail! Bail!"

James and John, "the sons of thunder," were probably doing their fair share of yelling and screaming too.

The wind was howling. The water was raging. The boat was pitching. It was noisy. Chaotic. And during the whole crisis, Jesus remained asleep in the stern.

How would you feel if you were in crisis and someone who supposedly loved you and was in the situation with you remained oblivious to your predicament?

When I was in the dire pain of labor, giving birth to my first son—long before the advent of the epidural—and my husband sat in the chair next to me, reading the sports section of the journal and munching on a bagel, I know how I felt!

I tore the newspaper from his hands and screamed, "I expect you to suffer with me!"

I was angry that I was suffering and he didn't seem to care.

I suspect that the reason the disciples woke Christ was that they felt the same way. They were upset that he was peacefully sleeping and not helping them bail. They wanted him to feel the same sort of panic that they felt.

They demanded, "Don't you care if we drown? Don't you see that we're in crisis? Why are you sleeping? Aren't you even the slightest bit concerned about our predicament?"

They didn't think Jesus was interested enough.

And how often do we think the same thing? We may believe that God is big enough, but we question whether he is interested in us enough to help.

Oh, he's interested in the pastor, or the missionaries, or our friend down the street. But is he really interested in me? we wonder. We conclude that it's up to us to look after number one. So, we rely on our own abilities and competency before asking him to intervene.

I've got this. No need to bother Jesus.

If someone were to have asked the disciples as they launched out in their boats that day if they trusted in Jesus, they would have undoubtedly responded with a resounding yes! But the storm revealed the truth.

Storms have a way of doing that.

The crisis revealed that they relied on themselves more than they relied on Christ. It revealed that their confidence was foolish and fragile.

When our trust is misplaced, our primary concern is gaining

control over the situation. But when our trust is Christ-centered, our primary concern is relinquishing control to the One who is truly in control.

That's why Philippians 4:6–7 instructs us, "Do not be anxious about anything, but in everything by prayer and supplication with thanksgiving let your requests be made known to God. And the peace of God, which surpasses all understanding, will guard your hearts and your minds in Christ Jesus."

Do not be anxious about anything!

I think of the long laundry list of things I'm anxious about today: Meeting my deadline. The election. COVID-19. My husband losing his job. Our finances. The water damage that needs fixing. My parents' health. The challenges facing my children and grand-children. The long list of to-dos that exceed my capacity.

Do not be anxious about anything.

How is that even possible?

The verse doesn't leave us hanging. It instructs, *but in every-thing let your requests be made known to God.*

Everything.

The deadline. The election. My parents' health. The renovation. COVID-19. My to-do list.

Everything.

The disciples' attitude of let's-just-take-care-of-this-ourselves-and-not-bother-Jesus indicated that they really didn't know him.

He *is* interested.

He *does* care.

He wants us to bring all our fears and anxieties to him. Even the smallest and seemingly most insignificant ones. Another verse puts it this way: "[Cast] all your anxieties on him, because he cares for you" (1 Peter 5:7).

There it is again. Another sweeping, all-encompassing statement. *All* your anxiety. Everything!

Do you think that storm took Jesus by surprise? No. He planned to use it as a training lesson—a confidence lesson, so to speak. The storm exposed what the disciples were putting their confidence in. It revealed that their source of confidence was fragile and inadequate. Most importantly, it challenged them to put their confidence in something infinitely greater and more reliable—Jesus!

God is your helper, even in the deepest, darkest, ugliest part of the mess. He is there even when you doubt his presence. He promises to stick with you through every trial: "Thus says the LORD, he who created you . . . 'Fear not, for I have redeemed you; I have called you by name, you are mine. When you pass through the waters, I will be with you; and through the rivers, they shall not overwhelm you; when you walk through fire you shall not be burned, and the flame shall not consume you. For I am the LORD your God'" (Isa. 43:1–3).

My eyes well up when I think of my friends who are currently being tossed about by megastorms. Nanette, whose son, daughter-in-law, and only two grandchildren were killed in a horrific, fiery car crash in Africa. Kimberly, whose husband has been suffering with excruciating and unrelenting neurological pain—and who was recently rocked with additional crises, adding to her pain, disappointment, and suffering. Nancy, who married a man whose wife died of cancer and is now facing the possibility of losing him to cancer. Jen, who is dealing with the fallout of abuse. Susan, whose son was just diagnosed with autism. Deb, whose husband left her after thirty years of marriage. I could go on.

The storms are fierce and relentless.

None of my friends would look at the magnitude of their problems and claim to have what it takes. They don't. Only God has the power to calm the storm and get them through to the other side. Hanging on to that promise through faith isn't always easy, but we can be certain that he will deliver us. "Many are the afflictions of the righteous, but the LORD delivers him out of them all" (Ps. 34:19).

The Lord is interested in every anxiety you feel and every crisis you face. When those waves hit your boat, you have a choice to make. You can react in panic and try to deal with the situation yourself, or you can turn to the Prince of Peace, relinquish control, and trust him to get you to the other side.

MISPLACED EXPECTATION: "GOD IS NOT GOOD ENOUGH."

The disciples had certain expectations of Jesus during that storm at sea. At the very least, they wanted him to demonstrate some alarm and concern. Perhaps they expected him to help bail water. Or maybe they hoped he'd multiply the buckets the way he'd multiplied the loaves of bread for the crowd on the hill. Maybe they expected him to supernaturally steady the pitching boat so they could row to shore.

It isn't clear what the disciples envisioned. But it is clear that Christ's response caught them totally off guard. He did not do what they expected.

God is not a personal genie to perform at our beck and call. Whenever we expect God to comply with our agenda—whenever we expect that he will do what we want, when we want, and how we want it—our expectation is misplaced.

When our expectation is misplaced, our primary concern is finding a positive short-term resolution to the situation. So often, we desperately fire some coins of prayer into the heavenly dispensing machine and feverishly push the button to indicate what we want from Jesus. We want the relationship saved, the sickness healed, the conflict resolved, the pain relieved, or the loss restored. We want the crisis averted. And we want it *now*!

Then we experience disappointment, disillusionment, and despair when God doesn't come through in the way we want. And we begin to question his goodness.

I know that God is big enough, and he tells me that he is interested enough, so I guess he is just not good enough. He likes seeing me suffer! He withholds from me what is in his power to give. Why?

Have you ever asked that question?

Years ago, a close friend of ours, Rusty, was diagnosed with cancer. He had a tumor the size of a sausage behind his stomach. The cancer had spread to his lymph nodes. The prognosis was not good.

At the time, Rusty was a young father with three preschool children. He had grown up without a father—his father had died when he was young. Having his children grow up without a father was one of Rusty's biggest fears.

Wow! What a storm!

We began to pray and throw ourselves on the mercy of God, begging him to heal Rusty. The surgeons removed as much of the tumor as they could. Then Rusty started the process of chemo and radiation.

We continued to pray and throw ourselves on the mercy of God, asking him to heal our friend.

After the first chemo treatment, Rusty began to sense that God had healed him. He knew it in his spirit. Nevertheless, he continued the prescribed course of intervention. Sure enough, on the fourth course of chemo, the oncologist informed him, "We haven't been able to find any traces of cancer the last three times you've come in."

There was not a trace of the tumor remaining. There was not a cancer marker to be found in his bloodwork. There was no cancer when they dissected his lymph nodes.

So they stopped treatment. That was more than twenty-five years ago. Rusty has been healthy and cancer-free ever since.

God miraculously healed him.

A few years after this amazing answer to prayer, another friend was diagnosed with the same kind of stomach cancer. Again, we began to pray and throw ourselves on the mercy of God. We wanted our friend Johnny to be healed as Rusty was.

But the cancer got worse.

Johnny's belly ballooned to an enormous size. His face and limbs wasted away. He went through excruciating pain and suffering.

We continued to pray and throw ourselves on the mercy of God, asking him to heal Johnny.

In the end, God did heal him—but not in the way we expected. Johnny went to be with the Lord and left behind a wife, two sons, and a young daughter.

So often we want to control God. But his ways are beyond ours. And we don't always understand them. But we can be assured that though he may not always do what we ask of him, he *is* good.

I asked Rusty to reflect on his journey with cancer and on the fact that he lived while Johnny died. Here is an excerpt from Rusty's email:

People have asked me why I was healed, and others, like our friend Johnny are not. Why?

I insist that this is the wrong question.

I think the "why" question is a question that is designed not to be answered. It is a question that reflects petulance, not faith. It is a question that really isn't expecting an answer, or at least one with which we will be satisfied.

I think the better question is "what" (and I think Johnny reflected this in his dying days).

"What now, Father?"

"What do I do now?"

"What are you doing with me?"

"What are you doing in and through this?"

The "what" question actually expects an answer. And indeed, I believe that's the whole point of difficulties: to ask our Father for direction and comfort during the time that we need it so desperately and to trust him.

"Why?" or "Why me?" is subversively saying, "You're wrong! I will not accept your sovereignty and wisdom! I question your goodness."

Some might say that it is easy for me to say this since I am, after all, still alive. But I insist that I'm just as ready to die now as I was back then. Therefore, I am really able to live!

I do not live in fear of diseases like cancer, or being kidnapped or killed in Colombia, or being eaten by a bear in Jasper. (Did I tell you we're going to the mountains on Thursday?)

As Paul said, "Whether I live or die, I live to Christ" [Rom. 14:8 paraphrase].

Johnny lived that out—I only hope to do the same. I am learning to live by faith; and to know that all I am and have belongs to our Father, who is both gracious and good.

God is good.

We do not always understand his ways. He does not always grant our requests in the way we would like. But nevertheless, he *is* good. And he loves us so very much.

Do you believe that God is good? Do you believe that he is good to you?

The apostle John stressed the importance of knowing and

believing the truth about God. He said, "So we have come to know and to believe the love that God has for us. God is love. . . . There is no fear in love, but perfect love casts out fear. For fear has to do with punishment, and whoever fears has not been perfected in love" (1 John 4:16, 18).

Perfect love casts out fear. The truth is this: God loves you and is on your side. You do not need to be afraid of God's punishment or displeasure. You can have confidence in his character. The more you know him, the more you will love him. The more you love him, the more you will understand his love for you. Perfect love will silence all the doubts you have about God. Reverent fear will cast out apprehensive fear.

When the disciples witnessed the power of Christ in calming the storm, their knees knocked. They felt megafear. Christ did not do what they expected. He is not tame. We cannot control him. When we follow Jesus, we can be in for a bit of a wild ride. As Mrs. Beaver warned Lucy in the Chronicles of Narnia, Aslan is not a tame lion.

That does not mean that we cannot ask him for help. God wants us to bring our requests boldly and expectantly before his throne (Matt. 7:7; James 4:2). The Lord wants us to pray constantly and fervently. We persistently knock on heaven's door, knowing that God longs to save relationships, heal sicknesses, resolve conflicts, relieve pain, and restore loss. He hears our cries, and he is "able to do far more abundantly than all that we ask or think" (Eph. 3:20).

So we ask. Not with the misplaced expectation that God *must* do what we want, how we want, when we want. But with the humble acknowledgment that he is God, and we are not. When we ask, we not only trust his power to heal and deliver but also trust his timing, his way, his wisdom, his sovereign right to rule, and his eternal purpose and plan.

UNSHAKABLE CONFIDENCE

The disciples learned a lot about confidence that night in the boat. Or, perhaps it would be more accurate to say that they learned a lot about Jesus. And that was the point, I suppose. In order to be confident, the disciples needed to grasp exactly who was riding in their boat. Jesus wanted them to know that he was stronger and more reliable than anything or anyone else they could put their confidence in. They needed a bigger view of who he was. They needed to rely on him more than they relied on other things.

It was the same for Moses. From a human perspective, who better to deliver the Hebrews from slavery than the strong, successful, self-confident adopted grandson of Pharaoh? No one could have been more qualified or better positioned. But God wanted Moses to learn that a blue-pill type of confidence is a facade. It's foolish and fragile. So, he stripped Moses of the things in which he trusted. Then, when Moses was emptied of all confidence in himself, God offered him the red pill.

Trust me.

It wasn't the self-reliant Moses but rather the humble, emptied-of-self, God-reliant Moses that God used to secure the Hebrews' deliverance. And that's usually the way God does things. Why? Because he wants us to have a red-pill, accurate view of reality. We need to know the truth about who he is and who we are in relation to him. When our hearts are gripped by a greater fear, all lesser fears will lose their grip.

Self-help confidence gurus say that in order to grow in confidence, you need to trust yourself more. But the Bible has a radically different take. It teaches that if you want to grow in confidence, you need to ditch the blue pill in favor of the red. You need to trust God more. You need to make him your confidence. You don't need a bigger view of self; you need a bigger view of God.

As we close this chapter, I want to make sure you take note of the confidence-building technique God used with both Moses and with the disciples: he allowed them to feel fear so they might learn to fear aright. He allowed their foolish, fragile confidence to be shattered so they could gain strong confidence in God. The disciples' fear was high-grade, intense panic. Moses' fear was low-grade, nagging insecurity. In both cases, the antidote to fear—and the prescription for strong confidence—was the fear of the Lord.

6

CONFIDENCE BUILDING

Every false support we lean on turns around and
bites us. . . . But Jesus never betrays our trust.

–Raymond Ortlund Jr.

The Niagara Falls are one of North America's most iconic natural wonders. The largest of the three falls—Horseshoe Falls—is the most spectacular waterfall in the Western Hemisphere. More than three-quarters of a million gallons of water thunder over its crest every second and crash down about sixteen stories into the roaring basin below.

Last year my husband and I took our youngest son to Niagara Falls for a special milestone birthday celebration. We did all the typical sightseeing things, including an excursion on the *Maid of the Mist* boat to the foot of the falls. Up close, pitching in the churning white water, and buffeted by the ferocious mist and spray, we got an even greater appreciation for the falls' mighty power.

This jaw-dropping experience provided context for the risky stunts we heard about at the IMAX Theatre *Niagara Daredevil Exhibit*. Over the years, numerous daredevils have ridden over the falls in barrels or homemade contraptions. Others have performed stunts on tightropes strung high above the imposing cascade.

The most well-known daredevil of Niagara Falls was a tightrope walker called "the Great Blondin." In 1859, he stretched a rope over a quarter of a mile to span the breadth of the Niagara gorge. Blondin was so confident in his own ability that he never used a net or safety harness—not even when crossing Niagara Falls. Effortlessly, he walked back and forth across the expanse. A huge crowd watched the stunning feat with shock and awe.

Blondin walked the tightrope at Niagara Falls on multiple other occasions. He crossed walking backward. He did somersaults and handstands. He walked across blindfolded and on stilts. He crossed on a bicycle. Once, he carried a stove and stopped in the middle to cook himself an omelet, then lowered the breakfast down on a rope for passengers on the *Maid of the Mist* to enjoy.[1]

The story of Blondin rolling a wheelbarrow across the tightrope at Niagara Falls is often cited by pastors as an illustration of what it means to have faith. You may have heard it. It is said that after pushing a wheelbarrow across the tightrope, Blondin asked the crowd if they believed he could push the wheelbarrow across with a person riding inside. The spectators enthusiastically cheered. *Yes.* They believed he could! But when Blondin asked, "Who will volunteer?" no one did. True belief, the illustration concludes, is more than just lip service. It means trusting the acrobat enough to actually climb in the wheelbarrow and go along for the ride.

Every illustration has its limitations. It's questionable whether putting confidence in a tightrope walker who wants to push you across Niagara Falls in a wheelbarrow is a smart thing to do. Even if Blondin successfully performed the feat a thousand times, there is no guarantee that he would be successful on the next time. Too much could go wrong.

Blondin's manager, Harry Colcord, had confidence in Blondin's abilities. He had witnessed Blondin safely walk tightropes all over the world. Therefore, Colcord agreed when Blondin proposed a stunt in which Blondin would carry him across Niagara Falls. As he traversed the tightrope with the terrified Colcord clinging to his back for dear life, several of the attached guy ropes unexpectedly snapped. The pair narrowly escaped disaster. The experience was so harrowing that Colcord vowed never to let Blondin carry him across a tightrope again.

Blondin's confidence paid off. His tightrope walking stunts earned him great fame and fortune. He kept performing well into his seventies. But two of his helpers were not as fortunate. They were killed when a tightrope snapped during one of his stunts. Nor did things always turn out well for the other performers who, like Blondin, confidently challenged Niagara Falls.

In 1887 Stephen Peer fell off a tightrope and was killed on the rocks below.

In 1920 Charles Stephens plunged over the falls in an oak barrel. The force of the water ripped the barrel apart. Stephens's right arm was the only part of his body that was recovered.

In 1990 expert whitewater kayaker Jessie Sharp tried to shoot the falls in his kayak. He was so confident of success that he made a dinner reservation for later that evening. He didn't show up. His kayak was discovered downstream. His body was never found.

In 1995 Robert Overacker attempted to go over the falls on a Jet Ski. The feat was unsuccessful. Bystanders watched in horror as

Overacker's parachute failed to open and he plunged to his death below.[2]

Confidence is of little value if your confidence is foolhardy or if the person or thing that you place your confidence in fails. If you want to have smart, strong confidence, you need to put your trust in the right place.

CONFIDENCE PROBLEM

Do you have a confidence problem? If you were to rate your confidence by putting an *X* on a scale of 0 to 10—with 0 being a *scaredy-cat* level of confidence (diffident, timid, fearful, flinching, unassertive, insecure, reluctant, doubtful) and 10 being *superconfident* (bold, courageous, daring, possessing backbone, determination, pluck, grit)—where would you place your *X*? Would you rank yourself more toward the diffident end of the scale or more toward the confident end of the scale? Why?

I'm a scaredy-cat. I have a confidence problem.

I'm superconfident. I don't have a confidence problem.

0 — 1 — 2 — 3 — 4 — 5 — 6 — 7 — 8 — 9 — 10

I struggle with a lot of things, but I generally don't struggle with feelings of inadequacy. I have an extremely strong "can-do" attitude. Just ask my kids. (Maybe it has something to do with my German heritage.) Therefore, I would rank myself quite high in confidence. I feel insecure from time to time, to be sure, and in some environments more than others, but those feelings pass quite quickly. They do not dominate my emotions, nor do they generally dictate my behavior. If someone were to ask, I would say that I do not have a confidence problem. I think I'd place my X at about an 8 or 9.

Lucky me, right?

Wait.

Not so fast.

Like me, you may view yourself as confident. You may think that because you don't struggle with insecurity, you don't really have a confidence problem. On the other hand, you may view yourself as a scaredy-cat. You feel timid and fearful most of the time. You may think that because you struggle with insecurity, you have a big confidence problem.

But before we conclude that the woman who feels confident doesn't have a confidence problem, and the one who doesn't feel confident does, let me ask you a slightly different question.

To what extent do you fully place your confidence in God?

I'm not talking about whether or not you've decided for Christ. I'm talking about the extent to which you rely on God on an ongoing daily basis. If you were to rate how much you trust God by putting an X on a scale of 0 to 10—with 0 being *no trust in God* (you trust yourself or other things and leave God out of the picture) and 10 being *complete trust in God* (you depend on God in everything at all times)—where would you put your X?

I leave God out of my day. I put my trust in other things.	I include God in all aspects of my day. I trust in him at all times.

0 — 1 — 2 — 3 — 4 — 5 — 6 — 7 — 8 — 9 — 10

It's a revealing question. And not an easy one to answer. I think I would place my *X* somewhere around 4. Sometimes, usually during a crisis, my trust meter might surge up much higher, and sometimes, when I get overly busy, my trust meter might dip even lower. If I am honest, I must admit that I fail to consistently put my trust in the Lord and often place my trust in myself or other things. Based on the second scale, I can see that I do have a confidence problem. And it may even be worse than those who rated themselves as scaredy-cats on the first scale.

I view myself as a confident woman, but if my confidence rests on a fragile, foolish source, it is worthless in God's eyes. You see, the Bible measures confidence an entirely different way. The strength of our confidence doesn't depend on a positive self-evaluation; it depends on the extent to which we trust God. We have a confidence problem whenever we put our trust in the wrong place.

When it comes right down to it, sin has messed up each one of us. We *all* have a confidence problem . . . whether we're aware of it or not.

Don't be fooled to think that because you don't struggle with insecurity you don't have a confidence problem. You undoubtedly have a confidence problem. You do, and I do too. The battle for our trust is fierce and relentless. Every day we must fight to reject the fragile, foolish type of confidence that Satan promotes and work to build the kind of confidence that God upholds as smart and strong. Whether we view ourselves as confident or insecure, we all need to learn to trust God more.

FIVE CONFIDENCE BUILDERS

So where do we begin? How do we build trust in order to become the strong, confident women God wants us to be? The following five confidence builders are a good place to start.

1. EXPAND YOUR VIEW OF GOD

Moses gained confidence when he learned who God was. Likewise, the disciples gained confidence when they gained a greater understanding of who Jesus was. To have strong confidence, these men didn't need a bigger view of self, they needed a bigger view of God. The Bible has scores of additional examples. We could talk about Gideon, Joshua, Caleb, Elijah, Elizabeth, Mary, and others. All of them gained confidence when they gained a proper perspective of God.

Sadly, most of us have a pathetically small view of God. We don't really believe that he is who he says he is, nor do we believe that he will do what he says he will do.

The overarching reason that Christians struggle with confidence is that we do not fully grasp who God is and who we are in relation to him. Virtually every problem we have with confidence can be traced back to that core issue. Therefore, the number one thing we can do to build strong confidence is to expand our view of God.

How? By meditating on God—who he is, what he says, and what he does.

That was David's secret.

According to David, the person who delights in God's Word and meditates on it day and night will be a genuinely happy—and confident—individual (Ps. 1:1–3). To meditate on something means to mull it over in your mind and think about it deeply.

David made a habit of meditating on Scripture. Psalm 119 indicates that he spent a lot of time pondering God's precepts (v. 15), statutes (v. 23), commandments (v. 48), law (v. 97), testimonies (v. 99), and promises (v. 148).

He spent a lot of time thinking about who God was too. In the book of Psalms, we learn that David meditated on God's greatness (77:13), holiness (29:2), love (48:9), justice (9:7), mercy (103:4), forgiveness (130:4), splendor and majesty (145:5), his spectacular beauty (27:4), and more.

David also pondered God's power (63:2) and God's mighty works and deeds (77:12). Night and day, God was at the forefront of his thoughts.

When he was a shepherd, David spent a lot of time outdoors, tending sheep. As he gazed up at the heavens, the moon, and the stars, he thought about what creation has to say about the nature and character of God (8:3; 97:6). "The heavens declare the glory of God, and the sky above proclaims his handiwork," David wrote (19:1).

God marks off the heavens with the span of his hand. He arranges the celestial objects with his fingers—all the clusters and superclusters, gamma ray bursts, planets, moons, nebulae, galaxies, comets, supernovae, quasars, pulsars, and black holes (8:3). It is he who determines the number of the stars and gives to all of them their names (147:4).

The sprawling Milky Way has an estimated one hundred billion stars. Scientists suggest that there are about two trillion galaxies in the observable universe, with hundreds of millions of stars in the average galaxy.[3] David didn't have insight into the size of the universe like scientists do today. But he did recognize that the heavens are bigger than he could fathom—and that God is even bigger than that (113:4; 150:1).

We know that everything that God created—from a star to a grain of sand—is composed of mini building blocks called molecules. Molecules contain even smaller building blocks called elements. Elements are chemical substances that are broken down to their simplest form, like hydrogen, carbon, and sodium.

The elements can be broken down into even tinier building blocks called atoms. Atoms are tiny—very tiny indeed. Atoms are so small that the period at the end of this sentence contains more than a billion of them. That's smaller than we can even imagine!

At one time, scientists believed that atoms were the smallest building blocks of matter. Now, they have discovered that atoms are made up of subatomic particles such as quarks, leptons, neutrinos, and hyperons. As scientists delve deeper into subatomic and particle physics, they discover more and more infinitesimal building blocks.

It's mind-boggling when you think about it.

David probably didn't know about molecules, elements, and atoms. Nevertheless, he recognized that everything—including his own body—was fearfully and wonderfully made, intricately woven together by God the Creator (Ps. 139:14–15).

As humans, we can't begin to comprehend the vastness of the universe, nor can we begin to comprehend its minuscule design. Creation is far more substantial and far more intricate than we could ever wrap our minds around.

The Bible testifies that the Lord is responsible for creating everything and for making everything work. He is the architect and sustainer of both the macro- and microcosmos: "He is before all things, and in him all things hold together" (Col. 1:17). "He upholds the universe by the word of his power" (Heb. 1:3).

What's even more jaw-dropping is that the same God who created and holds together each celestial supercluster and each tiny atom deeply cares for you and me. He assures us that his thoughts toward us are many and precious. Trying to number them would be like trying to count the grains of sand on a beach (Ps. 139:17–18).

God thinks about you constantly with deep affection. *This* God—who upholds the universe by the word of his power—says to you, *You are precious in my sight and honored, and I love you. Do not fear, for I am with you. I will hold you by your hand* (Isa. 41:10–13; 43:4–5).

Do you believe it?

The more you meditate on the truth found in God's Word, the more you will.

An accurate view of God is the starting point for building strong confidence. When you view God as big, your problems become small. As your reverent fear of him increases, so will your trust and confidence.

2. CHECK YOUR OVERCONFIDENCE AT THE DOOR

When I have an inadequate view of God, I view God as smaller than he actually is. This usually goes hand in hand with the opposite problem: I view myself as bigger than I actually am. Therefore, the second way to build confidence is to rid our hearts of a presumptuous, overconfident attitude.

The biblical word for overconfidence is *presumption*. What is presumption? Presumption is presuming that I know better than God. It's valuing my opinion as higher than his.

A presumptuous person exhibits a casual, disrespectful, irreverent attitude toward God. A callow, laid-back attitude.

She doesn't take God seriously.

Instead of reverently fearing God, she is far too easygoing with him. She shrugs off God's opinion the same way she might nonchalantly dismiss the opinion of a friend. She behaves in a way that shows a lack of respect by doing something that God says she has no right to do. Her thoughts are also audacious. She shows a lack of respect by doubting what God says is true.

Presumption is excessive self-confidence. Overconfidence, one might say, though ironically, it can manifest in a low view of self. For example, if God says he loves and accepts me, and I claim that he doesn't, then I am being presumptuous. I am setting my opinion up as higher than his.

Scripture tells us that a wicked man "puts on a bold face" or puts up a bold front (Prov. 21:29). He is overly sure of himself. He figures that he is thinking and doing the right thing. But his boldness is presumptuous. Disrespectful. Insolent. What's more, it is extremely sinful.

In the garden, Satan convinced Eve to presume that she knew more than God. Essentially, he convinced her to be overconfident. Self-confidently presuming that we know more than God is the attitude that lies at the root of all sin.

One of the most dramatic examples of the sin of presumption is the story of Uzzah and the ark of the covenant. The ark was the most sacred object in God's temple. It represented the very presence of God (1 Chron. 13:6).

We won't get into all the details, but during the days of Saul, the ark somehow ended up in storage at the house of Uzzah's father, Abinadab, where it gathered dust for decades. When David became king, he decided it was time to bring the ark back to Jerusalem and restore it to its rightful place in a tabernacle. David assembled everyone in Israel for the festive event. But his party didn't go as planned. Here's what happened:

> At Abinadab's house they set the ark of God on a new cart. Uzzah and Ahio were guiding the cart.
>
> David and all Israel were dancing with all their might before God with songs and with lyres, harps, tambourines, cymbals, and trumpets. When they came to Chidon's threshing floor, Uzzah reached out to hold the ark because the oxen had stumbled. Then the LORD's anger burned against Uzzah, and he struck him dead because he had reached out to the ark. So he died there in the presence of God.

David was angry because of the LORD's outburst against Uzzah, so he named that place Outburst Against Uzzah, as it is still named today. David feared God that day and said, "How can I ever bring the ark of God to me?" So David did not bring the ark of God home to the city of David; instead, he diverted it to the house of Obed-edom of Gath. (1 Chron. 13:7–13 CSB)

Worried that the ark was going to fall, Uzzah reached out his hand to steady it. And for his efforts, God struck him dead. Wow. Way to put a damper on David's party! Why would God do that? Especially since David was bringing the ark to where it belonged. What was the problem?

The problem was the overconfidence in Uzzah's heart. God saw some of the same attitude in David's heart. And also in the hearts of the partygoers. They had a casual view toward God—an irreverent view. The prophet Samuel explained, "Then the LORD's anger burned against Uzzah, and God struck him dead on the spot for his irreverence, and he died there next to the ark of God" (2 Sam. 6:7 CSB).

Uzzah died because he was irreverent.

Overconfidence caused him to treat the ark of God too casually.

God gave the Israelites explicit instructions about who could touch the ark and how it was supposed to be transported. Putting it on a cart was a big mistake. God clearly told the Israelites that the ark was not to be touched but only to be carried on poles, and only by Levites from the family of Kohath (Ex. 25:12–14; Num. 7:9). No matter how innocently it was done, touching the ark was a direct violation of God's holy law and was punishable by death.

Remember the old saying "familiarity breeds contempt"? Uzzah was so accustomed to the ark being in his house that he took it for granted. He was so accustomed to having it around that he began to view it as commonplace rather than holy.

Perhaps Uzzah was proud that the king acknowledged him as the ark's guardian. I imagine that having such a prominent position in the parade stoked his ego. Perhaps he viewed himself as Bobby Big Wheel. In any case, Uzzah reaching out to touch the ark was a presumptuous action that demonstrated irreverence toward God.

Did you notice how David reacted to Uzzah's death? He was *angry* at God. He figured that since he was doing so much for God, it wasn't fair for God to rain on his parade. The tragedy also caused David to *fear* God, but not in the right way. Not at first, anyhow. But David's heart slowly came around. He recognized that he and the people had indeed been presumptuous. And David repented of that attitude.

The next time David ordered the ark to be moved, he commanded the Levites to do it the right way—God's way (1 Chron. 15). It was a party that was more joyful, more exuberant, and more reverent than the first. At that party, David reminded the nation that they should always fear God and ascribe to God the glory and strength due his name. "For great is the LORD . . . he is to be feared above all gods" (16:25).

Presumption is an egregious sin. The Bible informs us that "presumption is as iniquity and idolatry" (1 Sam. 15:23). *Idolatry.* When I view my own opinions as weightier than God's, I set myself up as god. And that's just as offensive to him as worshiping a piece of carved wood or stone.

For example, God says no sex outside of marriage. If I sleep with my boyfriend anyhow, then I am being presumptuous. I am being overconfident in my own opinion. According to the Bible, that's not the right kind of confidence.

Are you presumptuous? Do you have a casual view toward God? Do you think you know better than he does? Do you ever shrug your shoulders and say, "I know what the Bible says, but I think . . ." Do you minimize the seriousness of sin? Do you indifferently and un-repentantly transgress his standards? Do you disregard him in your attitudes, your words, your actions, or your morals? Are you brash enough to disregard willfully and flagrantly what the almighty God says? Do you not fear God?

Some people think that Uzzah died because the God of the Old Testament was mean and angry. They think that God has changed. Now he never gets angry or upset. He's happy, regardless of what we do.

But wait.

What about Ananias and Sapphira?

That husband-wife duo were members of the early church. They sold a piece of property and brought some of the proceeds to the apostles. The trouble is, they led the apostles to believe they were giving *all* the monies from the sale. All they did was tell a little white lie to make themselves look bigger than they were. No big deal. No harm done. Right?

You know what happened. God struck them dead. The problem was not that Ananias and Sapphira didn't give the apostles all the money from the sale. It was theirs to give or keep. The problem was that they didn't take God seriously. They presumed that telling a little white lie was okay.

God freely forgives all our sins through Jesus Christ. We do not need to be afraid of his wrath or judgment. He showers us with his love and grace. But it is presumptuous to think that sin isn't a big deal. Or that we can shrug off God's instructions and do what we want.

Paul warned against this cavalier type of attitude. He asked, "Do you *presume* on the riches of his kindness and forbearance and patience, not knowing that God's kindness is meant to lead you to repentance?" (Rom. 2:4, emphasis added).

In order to build strong confidence, we need to fight against overconfidence. We need to constantly examine our hearts for that subtle I-know-better-than-God attitude.

All of us have a sinful tendency to value our own opinions above God's. But when it comes to confidence, this can land us in one of two opposite and equally dangerous ditches—the ditch of arrogance or the ditch of insecurity. We become arrogant when we think higher of ourselves than we ought to think. We become insecure when we think lower of ourselves than we ought to think.

To build strong confidence, we must humbly check our overconfidence at the door and let Christ renew our minds so that we can think about everything, including ourselves, the way that God says we should (Rom. 12:2–3).

3. CAST ASIDE YOUR FEAR OF PEOPLE

Confidence falters when we view people as big and God as small. The third way you can build confidence is to cast aside your fear of people.

The wise sage warned that fearing people is a dangerous attitude. "The fear of man lays a snare, but whoever trusts in the LORD is safe" (Prov. 29:25). The fear of man is like a spiked leg-hold trap that Satan sets to ensnare us.

It's dangerous. Fearing man more than we fear God is sure to do harm and trip us up.

A prime example is King Saul. The prophet Samuel was directed by God to anoint Saul as Israel's first king. Saul had a lot going for him. For starters, he was extremely good-looking. He was tall, dark, and handsome. If he had lived in our day, *People* magazine would have featured him on the cover of their "Sexiest Man Alive" issue. "There was not a man among the people of Israel more handsome than he. From his shoulders upward he was taller than any of the people" (1 Sam. 9:2).

But despite his good looks, Saul was terribly insecure. When Samuel first approached Saul to let him know that God had chosen him to be king of Israel, Saul objected, saying essentially, "I'm nobody! Why are you saying this?"

Samuel instructed Saul to watch for several supernatural signs that would confirm that he was God's choice. All the signs came to pass that day. But when Saul went home, he didn't tell anyone about his powerful encounter with God.

A week later, Samuel gathered all the people of Israel together to draw lots to select a king. The lot was drawn for Saul's tribe, clan, family, and then for Saul. But Saul was nowhere to be found. He had hidden himself among the baggage. The people had to forcibly haul him out from behind the storage chests to make him king.

Over time, King Saul proved himself to be a formidable military leader. He won the respect of his citizens and of foreign leaders. But somehow Saul never managed to get rid of the chip on his shoulder. Outwardly, he was a successful leader, but inwardly, he was plagued with insecurities. He feared people. He was anxious over what others thought of him. He wanted people to view him as impressive and admirable. But he was afraid they would see him as deficient instead.

Fear fueled Saul's jealousy and hatred of David. Fear fueled Saul's rage. Fear also fueled his disobedience. For example, before a battle against the Philistines at Gilgal, the prophet Samuel gave Saul explicit instructions not to begin the battle until Samuel arrived to offer a sacrifice (1 Sam. 13:8–12). But Saul was impatient. He was afraid of losing the battle and losing face. So instead of waiting for Samuel, he presumptuously presented the burnt offering himself.

Fear of man is ultimately what did Saul in.

The problem came to a head when Saul disobeyed God's instructions about how he should deal with the Amalekites, the archenemies of the Israelites (1 Sam. 15:1–4). Saul was supposed to destroy everything and not take any spoil—no cattle, no sheep, no treasure . . . nothing.

But Saul only partially obeyed.

Though he destroyed all the undesirable and worthless animals and goods, he let his men take the best plunder. Plus, he didn't kill the Amalekite king. He and his officers likely planned to put on a big show for the people back home. They intended to parade out the bounty and make a spectacle of the foreign king. They wanted to grandstand their illustrious victory.

Saul wanted the people to acknowledge him as being the best. So deep was his insecurity that he even "set up a monument for himself" after the victory to bolster his self-esteem (1 Sam. 15:12).

Samuel confronted Saul about his disobedience and he perceptively identified insecurity as the root of the problem. "You are little in your own eyes," Samuel observed (1 Sam. 15:17).

At first, Saul didn't acknowledge that he had done anything wrong. But when Samuel didn't let up, he admitted that he had disobeyed God because he feared people. "I have transgressed the commandment of the LORD and your words, because *I feared the people* and obeyed their voice" (v. 24, emphasis added).

Samuel reiterated that God was going to depose Saul as king, then turned to leave. Panicked, Saul grabbed hold of Samuel and begged him: "I have sinned; yet *honor me now before the elders of my people and before Israel,* and return with me, that I may bow before the Lord" (v. 30, emphasis added).

Do you see the problem with Saul's confession?

He was more concerned about his reputation—about being *honored* in front of the elders—than he was about his sin. Fearing people more than God cost Saul his kingship, his family, his faith, and ultimately his life.

Fear of people is Satan's trap.

It leads to sins of presumption, sins of comparison, and sins of cowardice.

As Jon Bloom said, "Being little in our own eyes can be either righteous or ruinous. It's righteous if we see God as big and us as small. This actually frees us from fear. But it's ruinous if the approval of man is what's big to us because it always leads to disobeying God."[4]

Fear of man *always* leads to disobeying God. What's more, it does nothing to build strong confidence. Our confidence is fragile indeed if it depends on what others think of us. Jesus instructed us to fear God and not people (Matt. 10:28–33). When we fear him, we need not fear them.

As David said,

> The Lord is on my side; I will not fear.
> What can man do to me?
> The Lord is on my side as my helper;
> I shall look in triumph on those who hate me.
> It is better to take refuge in the Lord
> than to trust in man.

> It is better to take refuge in the LORD
> than to trust in princes. (Ps. 118:6–9)

Your confidence will grow strong as you cast aside your fear of people and take your refuge in God instead. How can you do that? A good place to start is by memorizing Psalm 118:6–9 and quoting it the next time you feel the fear of people grip your heart.

4. STOP LEANING ON FRAGILE THINGS

Another way to build strong confidence is to stop leaning on fragile things. The Bible compares fragile, foolish confidence to a spider's web: "His source of confidence is fragile; what he trusts in is a spider's web. He leans on his web, but it doesn't stand firm. He grabs it, but it does not hold up" (Job 8:14–15 CSB).

One of the most important things we can do in our quest for confidence is to evaluate where we are placing our trust. What do we ultimately rely on for our sense of identity and security? Are we leaning on the Lord? Or are we leaning on a spider's web?

Just as a spider's web is composed of a network of individual threads, so confidence is based on a mesh of interrelated sources. A woman might place her confidence in her education, her job, her finances, her friends, her influence, or her looks. We all derive our confidence from a variety of things. The problem is that we can be fooled into thinking that these things are stronger and more reliable than God.

The things that most people rely on for confidence can be sorted into four basic categories. Or, to use the spiderweb imagery, the threads can be divided into four different quadrants: rank, rating, resources, and risk avoidance.

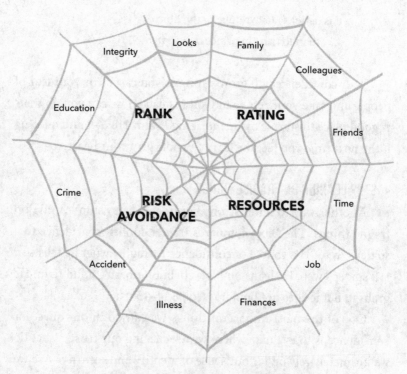

FIRST, MY RANK (PERSONAL EVALUATION): "I AM . . ."

Confidence: I am enough.

Fear: I am not enough.

The first quadrant covers the way I view myself. Some people would equate this with a personal sense of self-worth. I self-assess how I measure up. Am I strong or weak, capable or inept, smart or stupid, educated or uneducated, accomplished or unaccomplished, pretty or ugly, fun-loving or dull, personable or unlikable, hardworking or lazy, organized or disorganized, good or bad? If I think that I measure up to an acceptable standard, I feel confident. But if I think I don't measure up—that I'm not pretty enough, smart enough, or capable enough, for example—I feel insecure.

SECOND, MY RATING (GROUP EVALUATION): "THEY THINK I AM . . ."
Confidence: I will be accepted.
Fear: I will be rejected.

The second confidence quadrant has to do with how I think other people rate me. Do they view me as a good person? Do they think that I am smart and accomplished? If I think they have a positive view of me, I am more confident. But if I perceive that they have a negative view of me, my insecurity increases. I'm afraid that they will laugh at me, judge me, condemn me, or exclude me. I fear that I will be rejected and not accepted.

THIRD, MY RESOURCES (EVALUATION OF ASSETS): "I HAVE/DON'T HAVE . . ."
Confidence: I do not lack.
Fear: I lack.

Another quadrant from which I draw confidence is my resources. I take inventory to see what assets I have at my disposal. Assets like money, a job, possessions, time, connections, experts, advocates, or helpers. If I think I have everything I need, I will feel confident. But if I think I don't have what I need, I will feel apprehensive and afraid.

FOURTH, MY RISK AVOIDANCE (LIKELIHOOD OF LOSS/HARM): "WHAT IF . . ."
Confidence: I feel safe.
Fear: I feel unsafe.

The final quadrant of my confidence lattice is my ability to avoid a perceived risk. It's how vulnerable I feel to loss or harm.

What if something bad happens? What if I lose my job? What if my dream is shattered? What if something happens to a loved one? What if the election doesn't turn out the way I hope? What if I get sick? What if I die?

If I feel that the risk of loss and harm is low, I feel safe and confident. If I feel that the risk of loss and harm is high, I feel unsafe and fearful. Risk avoidance relates to my sense of control over future events—that is, my perceived ability to keep something bad from happening or my ability to mitigate a potential loss.

The reason so many women lack confidence is because they know that their source of confidence isn't strong. It's highly fragile. The threads on which they pin their hope could give way at any moment. And no amount of pumping up their tires with self-esteem or positive feelings will change that fact.

The Bible teaches that in the grand scheme of things, all humans are puny and insignificant—even those who appear strong and powerful. Psalm 62:9 tells us that "those of low estate are but a breath; those of high estate are a delusion; in the balances they go up; they are together lighter than a breath." Psalm 39 points out that all the earthly things on which we depend can be consumed like a moth-infested stack of sweaters (v. 11).

Scripture urges us to stop relying on human strength and competency as it is essentially worthless (Isa. 2:22). If we want strong confidence, we need to rely on something far more reliable than this world has to offer.

Human strength is an illusion.

The spiderweb is fragile.

Leaning on it is foolish.

I love the spiderweb analogy the Bible uses. To me, the imagery is rich. You see, I have a lot of experience with spiderwebs. We have a rustic family cabin at a remote lake in Northern Canada. Every summer, while my husband battles the ants, I battle the spiderwebs.

Those spiders work twenty-four-seven to put up webs. They spin webs on the chairs, on the table, on the volleyball net, on the strings of patio lights, on the stack of firewood, on the doors, on the windows, in the boathouse, in the outhouse. They spin webs literally *everywhere*. Every corner, nook, and cranny. So each time we arrive at the cabin, I have to pull out the old straw corn broom to knock down the spiderwebs. Otherwise we'd be overrun with translucent sticky gauze.

Knocking down spiderwebs with the corn broom doesn't take long. The webs are fragile and easy to destroy. But the battle is relentless. I can have everything cleaned up one day only to have a whole new crop of webs appear the next morning. Sometimes the webs are massive. And with the dew glistening on each fragile line of silk, they can look spectacular. I am often wowed by the spider's skill and tenacity.

The reason I love the analogy of false, foolish confidence being like a spider's web is because it so aptly describes the ongoing battle of trust in my own heart. The temptation to trust in my own ability and resources crops up constantly. Every day I need to evaluate whether I am leaning on God or on a web of other things. The Lord says, "Do not turn aside after empty things that cannot profit or deliver, for they are empty" (1 Sam. 12:21).

As the old hymn says:

> *What have I to dread, what have I to fear,*
> *Leaning on the everlasting arms?*
> *I have blessed peace with my Lord so near,*
> *Leaning on the everlasting arms.*
> *Leaning, leaning,*

> *Safe and secure from all alarms;*
> *Leaning, leaning,*
> *Leaning on the everlasting arms.*[5]

What things do you lean on? What sources of human strength would you list on the quadrants of your confidence web? Your confidence will grow strong as you stop leaning on a fragile web and start to lean on God's everlasting arms.

5. AVOID CHASING THE BUZZ

Confidence experts evaluate the strength of a person's confidence on how confident that person feels. Therefore, they aim to help women drum up more sunny, positive, affirmative feelings about their ability to succeed. Their job is done when the women *feel* like superconfident women.

The problem with equating confidence with a feeling is that feelings aren't indicative of whether a person's confidence is smart or foolish, strong or fragile. Every single daredevil who took on Niagara Falls felt confident that he or she would live to tell the tale. Blondin's feeling of confidence gained him fame and fortune. But the confident feelings of the other daredevils only landed them in a world of hurt.

It's important for you to understand that what the world promotes as confidence is merely the feeling or illusion of confidence. It's imaginary. It's not the real deal. "A rich man's wealth is his strong city, and like a high wall *in his imagination*" (Prov. 18:11, emphasis added). According to the Bible, the strength of your confidence depends on the strength of the object of your trust, not on the strength of your feeling.

To build strong confidence, you need to avoid chasing the buzz.

We chase the buzz when we equate strong confidence with a strong *feeling* of confidence. This idea is dangerous because it encourages us to chase the illusive buzz instead of working to put our trust in the right place. The buzz is deceptive. A strong buzz may convince us that our confidence is strong when it is actually weak. A weak buzz may convince us that our confidence is weak when it is actually strong.

Moses is a good example. By all accounts, forty-year-old Moses was a superconfident guy. He felt confident that he could help liberate the Hebrew people from Egyptian slavery. He certainly appeared to be the person for the job. He had the smarts, the skills, the power, and the position. But when his attempt failed, his confidence shattered. Fast-forward forty years and Moses was a quivering, insecure mess. He did not feel confident at all.

From a human standpoint, forty-year-old Moses' confidence was strong, while eighty-year-old Moses' confidence was weak.

But that's not the way God sees things.

Regardless of how Moses felt—confident or insecure—he was putting his "eggs" in the wrong basket. It's irrelevant how full that basket was. Regardless of whether it was full or empty, it was still the wrong basket. Moses' feelings had nothing to do with the strength of the source in which he was placing his trust.

The problem was not that forty-year-old Moses was overconfident and eighty-year-old Moses lacked confidence. The problem, in both instances, was that he was misplacing his trust. Moses wasn't putting his trust in God. He was banking on the wrong kind of confidence.

We often view confidence as a feeling. When we feel good about our ability to succeed, we conclude that our confidence is strong. But when we feel doubtful or fearful about our ability to succeed, we conclude that our confidence is weak. We equate having strong confidence with a positive, optimistic feeling about our chance of success. Often, when we seek confidence, what we are really seeking is the buzz—the feeling or illusion of confidence.

The Bible puts confidence on an entirely different grid. The strength of your confidence doesn't depend on how confident you *feel*—it depends on whether your confidence is placed in Jesus Christ, the rock-solid source of confidence. If you rely on God more than other things, you will have strong, smart confidence. If you rely on other things more, your confidence will be fragile and foolish. When you pursue strong confidence, you are not pursuing a feeling—you are resolving to put your trust in the right basket. How confident you *feel* has little to do with it.

Earlier in this chapter, I asked you to rate your confidence on a scale of 0 to 10. I rated myself at about an 8 or 9. That's because I generally feel confident. Then I asked you to rate the extent to which you place your confidence in God on a daily basis. On this scale, I only rated myself at about a 4. The point of this exercise was to show you that it is possible to *feel* confident and yet *misplace* your confidence.

The Bible is concerned about your *source* of confidence and its actual strength rather than on how certain or uncertain that source makes you feel. I cannot stress this point enough.

Some women feel extremely good about the web of things they depend on. Their spiderweb is intricately constructed with threads of personal competence, money, beauty, education, position, relationships, and influence. These women exude confidence. They are confident that their web is strong enough to hold them up. It's only when a sudden storm threatens their web that they see how fragile their source of confidence actually is.

Others feel insecure about the web of things on which they depend. Like nail-biting, nervous Moses, they feel that they are not enough. They compare their own spiderweb to the ones their neighbors are weaving and conclude that their own is inadequate. They lack the capacity, the resources, and the wherewithal to succeed. These women envy the woman with the bigger, prettier, more spectacular network of resources. Riddled with insecurities, these women figure the only way they can grow more confident is to somehow get a bigger and better web. Yet they despair that even if they do, it will still not be enough.

The point is this: Whether we feel insecure or confident—or even superconfident, filled with bravado—in God's eyes, our feelings are not the most important thing. The thing that truly matters is *where* we are placing our trust. And that is something we all ought to examine.

Do not be deceived. Confidence is not wrapped up in a feeling. It's wrapped up in the person of Jesus Christ. He is our strong confidence.

Can Jesus help us feel more confident? Can putting our trust in him alleviate our feelings of fear and insecurity? Yes, absolutely. But chasing the feeling is like chasing the gift rather than the giver. Feelings come and go. But if you put your trust in God, "The LORD will be your confidence and will keep your foot from being caught" (Prov. 3:26).

IT ALL COMES BACK TO FEAR

In this chapter, we explored five barriers to strong confidence. As I said at the outset, every problem we have with confidence can be traced back to one core issue: failing to fully grasp who God is and who we are in relation to him. A confidence problem is a fear problem; a problem we have with rightfully fearing God.

The good news is that the Bible makes it clear that the fear of God is far more than an emotion; it is something that can be *taught* and *learned*.

David was intentional about teaching people how to fear God: "Come, O children, listen to me; I will teach you the fear of the LORD" (Ps. 34:11).

God said, "Gather the people . . . so that they may listen and learn to fear the LORD your God" (Deut. 31:12 CSB). He also said, "Let them hear my words, so that they may learn to fear me all the days that they live on the earth, and that they may teach their children so" (4:10).

God gives you everything you need to grow in the reverent fear of the Lord. He gives you truth through his Holy Bible. He gives you power through his Holy Spirit. He gives you support through his holy church. Therefore, you have everything you need to build strong confidence.

Today would be a good day to pick up that corn broom and start.

7

DEEPLY ROOTED CONFIDENCE

'Twas grace that taught my heart to fear,
and grace my fears relieved.

—John Newton, "Amazing Grace"

Earlier this year, scientists in Israel announced that they have successfully grown extinct date palm trees from ancient seeds found at archaeological sites in the Judean Desert.

In the Holy Land, date palms were so abundant the Greeks and Romans called it "the land of the palms." Dates were a staple crop in Israel. Thick forests of date palms covered the Jordan River valley from the Sea of Galilee in the north to the shores of the Dead Sea in the south. However, when Rome destroyed the city of Jerusalem and its temple in AD 70, it also destroyed the date palms. Roman armies razed the trees in an attempt to cripple the Jewish economy. The remaining palms were destroyed in subsequent conquests. By the time the Jews resettled Israel in 1948, the once plentiful date palm was extinct.

The dates exported by Israel today are harvested from trees that were imported from Iraq and Morocco in the early part of the last century. They are not the same trees or the same dates that flourished in ancient times.

You can imagine how excited archaeologists were to discover a small stockpile of date palm seeds stored in a clay jar among the ancient ruins of Masada—not to mention when a botanical researcher successfully germinated the first seed in 2005.

She dubbed the sapling Methuselah.

After the success with Methuselah, botanists carefully planted dozens more of the rare two-thousand-year-old seeds. Six more saplings sprouted: Adam, Jonah, Uriel, Boaz, Judith, and Hannah. After several years, Hannah flowered, and botanists successfully fertilized her with Methuselah's pollen.

In 2020, for the first time in more than a millennium, Jewish botanists harvested the sweet fruit of the same type of palm that grew in Bible times.[1]

LIKE A PALM OR CEDAR

The Israeli date palm is fascinating. Especially since it's one of the trees the Bible uses to illustrate how we flourish when our confidence is deeply rooted in the Lord.

Scripture compares the right kind of confidence to a deeply rooted tree, and the wrong kind of confidence to a desert shrub.

> Thus says the LORD:
> "Cursed is the man who [puts confidence] in man
>   and makes flesh his strength,

whose heart turns away from the LORD.
He is like a shrub in the desert,
and shall not see any good come.
He shall dwell in the parched places of the wilderness,
in an uninhabited salt land.

"Blessed is the man who trusts in the LORD,
whose [confidence] is the LORD.
He is like a tree planted by water,
that sends out its roots by the stream,
and does not fear when heat comes,
for its leaves remain green,
and is not anxious in the year of drought,
for it does not cease to bear fruit." (Jer. 17:5–8)

To the Jews, the contrast was extremely meaningful. They were well acquainted with the difference between a bush that grew in the wilderness and a tree that grew beside a desert oasis.

On a trip to Israel a few years ago, I was surprised to discover that the desert in Israel is far different than the flat, sandy terrain of the Sahara. Israel's desert isn't exactly flat. It's comprised of limestone and gypsum plateaus, craters, and cliffs. It isn't exactly sandy either. It's rocky and dusty. And it isn't dotted with flora and fauna, like deserts in California. The desert in Israel is stark and hauntingly bare, especially around the Dead Sea. There, the high concentration of minerals and salts prevent everything from growing. It's one of the most eerily barren places on our planet.

So, when God told the Israelites that the person who put their confidence in mortals was like a shrub in an "uninhabited salt land," they undoubtedly got the picture. A few small bushes might spring up in regions of the wilderness that were sufficiently far away from the salt of the Dead Sea. But those bushes certainly wouldn't be lush and green. They'd look more like brittle, dried-up tumbleweeds. They'd be barren, stunted, and pathetic looking.

Juxtaposed against this bleak, lifeless image is the person who puts his or her trust in God. That person "is like a tree planted by streams of water that yields its fruit in its season, and its leaf does not wither. In all that he does, he prospers" (Ps. 1:3).

The image that would have come to mind for the Jews is a spring like Gan HaShlosha, the Park of the Three (Springs). That place is so beautiful that some rabbis claim it is a remnant of the garden of Eden. The pools and waterfalls are filled with deep, emerald-blue water. The crystal water is constantly refreshed by natural underground springs. Flowers and other vegetation crowd around the banks, as do the graceful date palms, which grow tall to provide shade from the hot sun.

Date palms grow to forty, fifty, even eighty feet in height. Feathery green fronds—up to twenty feet long—crown the trunk. The fibers of the tree are extremely elastic. Thus, the tree trunk bends but does not break with the force of the wind.

The date palm is both beautiful and useful. It begins to bear fruit about five years after being planted, producing more than three hundred pounds of dates annually. It continues to be productive for more than a century; and as the tree grows older, the fruit gets sweeter.

In antiquity, dates grown in Israel were famous for their large size, sweet taste, long storage life, and high nutritional value. What's more, they were renowned for medicinal properties not found in modern varieties. Ancient dates served as a cure for a wide range of maladies including cancer, malaria, and toothaches. The dates were so highly valued that King Herod annually sent a gift of Israeli dates to the Roman emperor.

But the date palm's importance to Israel was far greater than its nutritional, medicinal, or trade value. The tree was most cherished for its deep religious symbolism.

The date palm is a symbol of God's blessing. The fronds are a symbol of victory. Date palms were featured abundantly in both Solomon's temple and in Ezekiel's vision of God's eternal dwelling place. At Jesus' triumphal entrance into Jerusalem the crowd enthusiastically waved palm fronds.

When God said that people who put their confidence in him flourish like a palm, the image is one of lasting spiritual strength, victory, beauty, and fruitfulness.

David added that those who put their confidence in God grow like a cedar in Lebanon. This imagery is also powerful. Lebanon is the mountain range marking the northern boundary of the promised land. The Lebanese mountains were famous for their cedar forests, which were called "the glory" of Lebanon (Isa. 35:2). To this day, the Lebanese flag prominently features the image of a cedar tree.

The Lebanese cedar is a magnificent, deep-rooted evergreen tree that grows for as many as two thousand years. It can reach massive diameters and heights (up to 130 feet).[2] Its fragrant wood is red in color and is highly resistant to insects and decay. The wood is highly esteemed for its beauty and durability.

Cedar was an important trade item. King David used cedar in his palace. King Solomon imported panels of cedar for building his palace and the temple in Jerusalem. The Egyptians imported cedar for the tall, straight masts of their ships and for the durable coffins of their dead. King Nebuchadnezzar used cedar extensively for construction in his Babylonian Empire.

The Hebrew word for cedar comes from a root word meaning "firm."[3] The cedar is referenced dozens of times in the Bible as a symbol of spiritual strength and longevity, for the tree stands eternally strong and tall.

The quality of the cedar that is most impressive is its root system. The roots of this magnificent tree extend below ground as far as its branches extend above ground, making the tree immovable.[4] Some people estimate that the root of the Lebanese cedar grows three feet into the ground for every foot the tree grows up above ground.[5] Regardless of whether or not this ratio is accurate, it is undeniable that Lebanese cedar roots grow deep to make the tree grow firm and strong.

God says his people are like that. They "take root like the cedars of Lebanon" (Hos. 14:5 CSB).

Regardless of whether the Bible uses the imagery of a cedar or of a palm, the point is the same: a woman who puts her confidence in God is "like a tree planted by water, that sends out its roots by the stream" (Jer. 17:8).

The New Testament unpacks the imagery even further. It reveals that we have confidence when we are rooted in Christ and send our roots down deep to draw nourishment from *his* stream (Col. 2:6–7). He provides his followers with "living water"—the gift of his indwelling Holy Spirit (John 4:14; 7:39).

Thus, if you have put your trust in Jesus, God has given you a source of confidence that is greater and more reliable than any earthly power. You need not beg for this confidence. You already possess it. It is yours.

It is rooted in you; you are rooted in it.

This source of confidence doesn't originate with you, nor does it depend on you. It is supernatural. It will never dry up or be depleted. It flows inside of you like a moving stream. It is alive and active. Imperishable. Eternal.

Most importantly, this confidence is not out of reach. It is near.

It is in your heart so that you can access it. God promises you will grow as bold and strong as a date palm and cedar when you send your roots deep into this supernatural source.

What an amazing metaphor.

And what an amazing promise!

FLIPPING THE *V*

Placing our confidence in God means placing our trust in unseen things. We can't see a spiritual root. We can't see living water. We can't measure it. We can't snap a selfie with it to post to our feed. We can't wrap it up in pretty paper and a bow. We can't compare how much we have to how much our neighbor has.

It's much easier to place my trust in things that I can see. Like the income listed on my tax return, the degree hanging on my wall, the number of followers on my social media feed, the clean bill of health from my doctor, or the reflection in my mirror.

Scripture warns that if I lean on this web, it will not stand firm. If I grab it, it will not hold up. Trusting in earthly things is foolish. I ought to place my trust in God instead.

Throughout this book we've talked about the Bible's confidence code:

RELYING ON GOD > RELYING ON OTHER STUFF = STRONG/SMART CONFIDENCE
RELYING ON GOD < RELYING ON OTHER STUFF = FRAGILE/FOOLISH CONFIDENCE

Whether we have strong, smart confidence or fragile, foolish confidence depends on the direction of that *V*. It depends on the source of our strength.

Fragile confidence cuts God out of the picture. It relies on created things but denies the One who created them. The reason fragile confidence is so flimsy is that it separates the invisible from the visible. In doing so, it cuts off the tree from its roots. The roots are the most vital part of a tree. A tree without roots is no longer a tree—it's just a piece of dead wood.

As Paul said, "We do not focus on what is seen, but on what is unseen. For what is seen is temporary, but what is unseen is eternal" (2 Cor. 4:18 CSB). Paul's focus—his attention, hope, and security—was firmly directed toward unseen, eternal things.

Connecting the visible to the invisible impacts our worldview. It radically reorients our perspective toward all the things in which we might place our trust.

Let's consider how bringing God into the picture impacts each quadrant of our confidence web.

RANK: WHAT I THINK OF MYSELF

Paul rhetorically asked people who were strutting their stuff, "What do you have that you did not receive? If then you received it, why do you boast as if you did not receive it?" (1 Cor. 4:7).

When I connect the seen to the unseen, I acknowledge that "every good gift and every perfect gift is from above, coming down from the Father of lights" (James 1:17). Everything is "from him and through him and to him" (Rom. 11:36). It's all about God.

I understand that all my personal attributes—my smarts, looks, and abilities—come from God. He created me. He gives me "life and breath and *everything*" (Acts 17:25, emphasis added).

King David understood this.

David was a skilled fighter. He undoubtedly trained hard and kept his body in good physical condition. I'm sure he had a pretty good idea about how much weight he could lift, how fast he could run, what he could do with a sword, and how likely he was to hit the bull's-eye with a bow and arrow. Yet David recognized that everything he had came from God. What's more, he recognized that God could even give him ability that supernaturally exceeded his natural human ability. "For by you I can run against a troop, and by my God I can leap over a wall" (Ps. 18:29).

Connecting the seen to the unseen has profound implications for the way we view our personal competencies and inadequacies. If I humbly acknowledge that God is my Creator, I recognize that he is behind my abilities and accomplishments. He is the One who should get the glory.

Paul made a habit of giving credit where credit was due. He chalked up all his accomplishments to the power of Christ working through him. He said, "In Christ Jesus, then, I have reason to be proud of my work for God. For I will not venture to speak of anything except what Christ has accomplished through me" (Rom. 15:17–18).

What about our inadequacies? What about those of us who feel we are lacking in smarts, looks, or abilities or in some other way?

Moses was insecure about speaking up in front of a crowd. When he complained to God that he was not good with words, God asked him, "Moses, who made your mouth?" The answer, of course, was that God made his mouth. And God doesn't make mistakes!

Moses viewed his inadequacy as a liability. But God viewed it as an opportunity to showcase his glory. In God's eyes, inadequacies aren't liabilities; they are opportunities for God to prove himself strong.

Like Moses, Paul suffered with some sort of personal deficiency. We don't know what it was. It may have been a problem with speaking or some sort of physical ailment. Regardless of what it was, Paul viewed it as a liability.

Paul described the inadequacy as his thorn in the flesh (2 Cor. 12:7). In other words, this shortcoming really irked him. He repeatedly prayed for God to take it away. But God didn't. Instead, the Lord promised Paul that God's grace would be sufficient for him and that God's power would be made perfect in his weakness.

To God, shortcomings aren't liabilities; they are opportunities.

"Therefore," concluded Paul, "I will boast all the more gladly of my weaknesses, so that the power of Christ may rest upon me" (v. 9).

Do you struggle with feelings of inadequacy?

Do you ever feel as though you are not enough?

Strong confidence does not rest on human ability, nor is it crippled by human inability. Our Creator uses both for his glory. In God's eyes, each one of us is enough. We can be confident that we are sufficient in him. "Such is the confidence that we have through Christ toward God. Not that we are sufficient in ourselves to claim anything as coming from us, but our sufficiency is from God" (2 Cor. 3:4–5).

RATING: WHAT OTHERS THINK OF ME

As we saw in the last chapter, the fear of people is a major barrier to strong confidence. However, when we tip the *V* in the confidence equation the proper direction, we rely on what God thinks of us more than what people think of us. We base our confidence on what he says rather than on what they say.

God has a lot to say about who you are in Christ. For starters, he says you are

- firmly rooted (Col. 2:7),
- welcomed and accepted (Rom. 15:7),

- dearly loved (Col. 3:12),
- a new creation (2 Cor. 5:17),
- blessed with every spiritual blessing (Eph. 1:3),
- a recipient of God's lavish grace (Eph. 1:6–8),
- complete (Col. 2:10),
- a child of light (1 Thess. 5:5), and
- God's delight (Zeph. 3:17).

Do you believe it? Do you *really* believe it?

These are God's words about you. Not mine. When God looks at you, he does not evaluate you the way that people do. He does not judge you based on your abilities or shortcomings. He does not base his feelings on how pretty, talented, rich, or popular you are.

He sees who you are in Christ.

Your identity in Christ ought to be a source of deep confidence. For if the almighty God of the universe says these things about you, what does it matter what mere mortals think?

Not only does placing our confidence in Jesus address our fear of what people *think* of us, it also addresses our fear of what they *do* to us.

It's undeniable that people can do us harm.

They can harm us emotionally, financially, or physically. We can be misrepresented, slandered, or attacked. We can face public ridicule, social ostracism, or even unjust legal retribution.

The fear of people is definitely not without cause. Church history is laced with stories of Christian brothers and sisters who were mocked, slandered, imprisoned, tortured, and put to death for their faith. More than seventy million Christians have been martyred in the course of history. Even now, the persecution of those who follow Jesus is increasing around the world.

Each month around the world 322 Christians are killed for their faith, 214 churches and Christian properties are destroyed, and 772 forms of violence, such as beatings, abductions, rapes, forced marriages, and arrests are committed against Christians.[6] We are naive, indeed, if we think that this could never happen in the United States or that it couldn't happen to us.

Most of you are not facing persecution for your faith, but some of you are undoubtedly facing heartache and hardship because of what an opponent has done—or is trying to do—to hurt you. Scripture tells us that when enemies attack, fear can be quieted by placing our confidence in the Lord. As David said,

> The LORD is my light and my salvation;
>   whom shall I fear?
> The LORD is the stronghold of my life;
>   of whom shall I be afraid? . . .
> Though an army encamp against me,
>   my heart shall not fear;
> though war arise against me,
>   yet I will be confident. (Ps. 27:1, 3)

David also wrote, "In God I trust; I shall not be afraid. What can man do to me?" (Ps. 56:11). He was not saying that mortal man was incapable of inflicting harm. His point was that God would keep him safe in the only way that mattered. David's eternal standing and future were secure. Of that he was confident.

God's divine affirmation and protection are eternal and unshakeable for those who trust in Jesus Christ. His power is greater than any mortal foe.

Do you struggle with the fear of man? Maybe this fear crops up in your heart because you feel insecure about what people might think of you. Or maybe you are frightened by circumstances orchestrated by someone who is bent on doing you harm. Regardless of the circumstance, the Bible encourages you to put your trust in God. He will lead and protect you.

"In God I trust; I shall not be afraid. What can flesh do to me?" (Ps. 56:4).

RESOURCES: THE ASSETS I HAVE AT MY DISPOSAL

David and his men were ready to go to battle. But before they left, he gathered everyone together for a parting worship service. After the priests prayed and asked God for victory, David confidently declared, "I know that the LORD saves his anointed; he will answer him from his holy heaven with the saving might of his right hand. Some trust in chariots and some in horses, but we trust in the name of the LORD our God" (Ps. 20:6–7).

Does that mean that David went into battle without chariots and horses? Did trusting God mean that he did not make use of this type of military equipment?

Of course not.

David may not have had as many chariots and horses as his enemies, but he probably took what he had into battle. The point wasn't whether or not he had chariots; the point was whether he relied on them for victory. David believed that victory depended on God, not on the size and quality of the army or the military equipment (Ps. 33:16–22).

Relying on God does not mean rejecting the resources that God puts at our disposal. We rely on God when we recognize that everything comes from him, when we give him our best effort, when we lean on him for supernatural help, and when we trust him with the outcome. Putting confidence in God means keeping God at the center of the whole situation.

It's tempting to place our confidence in material resources. If we think we have enough—a good job, a house, money, clothing, possessions, health insurance, and the right experts to help us out—we feel secure. But if we think we don't have enough, we feel apprehensive and afraid.

When COVID-19 hit, my husband, like many others, lost his job. All our careful financial planning flew out the window, and we were forced to dip into our savings. When something like that happens, we can begin to worry. *Where will we get the money to pay our mortgage? How will we make ends meet? Will we have enough?*

The Bible talks a lot about putting our trust in God and not in money and material resources. It assures us that we don't ever need to worry about our needs being met. For God "will supply every need of yours according to his riches in glory in Christ Jesus" (Phil. 4:19). God is rich. He owns everything. Therefore, we can be confident that we will always have enough. Jesus stressed that because God is our Father, we don't need to be anxious about our daily needs.

> Don't strive for what you should eat and what you should drink, and don't be anxious. For the Gentile world eagerly seeks all these things, and your Father knows that you need them. But seek his kingdom, and these things will be provided for you. Don't be afraid. (Luke 12:29–32 CSB)

Is there anything you need God's provision for today?

God delights to meet our needs. He will make all grace abound to you, so that you have *all* sufficiency in *all* things at *all* times (2 Cor. 9:8). The Bible is adamant that those who know him can put their confidence in him, for he will never forsake those who seek him (Ps. 9:10).

I think of the example of George Mueller. He was one of the founders of the Plymouth Brethren movement in the 1800s. During his lifetime he cared for more than 10,000 orphans. He established 117 schools that offered Christian education to more than 120,000 children. George is famous for his confidence in God to provide what his orphanages needed.

Once, an orphanage had no food. Nevertheless, George instructed three hundred orphans to sit down in the dining room around the table and give thanks for the food they were about to receive. Then they waited. George didn't know where the food would come from, but he was certain it would come.

God had provided a building to house the orphans. He had provided caregivers, furniture, clothing, and food. Whenever George prayed about their needs, answers came. The money, supplies, or food often came at the last minute, but God never let him down. And so they waited.

Within minutes, a baker knocked on the door with several batches of bread. Soon there was another knock. A milk cart had broken down in front of the orphanage. The milkman needed to dispose of the milk so he could fix the wheel. Could they, by any chance, make use of it? George smiled. There was just enough milk to meet the needs of the thirsty children.[7]

George was so confident that God would answer that he thanked God for the provision even before it arrived. Your needs may be different from the needs of those orphans. But you can be sure that God will supply all your needs too.

As the wise sage noted, "I have been young, and now am old, yet I have not seen the righteous forsaken or his children begging for bread" (Ps. 37:25). With God, you can be confident that you will always have enough.

RISK AVOIDANCE: MY ABILITY TO AVOID POTENTIAL LOSS OR HARM

Have you ever worried about what might happen in the future? I think all of us do. We worry about the potential job loss, health crisis, relationship breakdown, natural disaster, election outcome, or any number of other what-if worst-case scenarios. We fret, worry, and lay awake at night speculating on what might happen.

The book of Proverbs says that the woman who fears the Lord smiles at the future. She laughs at the days to come (Prov. 31:25). Because she fears God, she isn't afraid of all those what-ifs. She is confident that the Lord will be with her no matter what tomorrow might bring.

Nighttime seems to be the time when all those what-ifs run wild. How often have you lain awake at night with worry, going through all sorts of what-if scenarios in your mind?

Psalm 4 is a nighttime psalm that David prayed when he was on the run from his son Absalom. The situation that was unfolding was not good. David's own son was leading a conspiracy against him (2 Sam. 15:1–18:33). Can you imagine? Just think of the fears and worries and what-ifs that must have plagued David's mind.

The psalm reflects how David stilled his churning thoughts. He focused on what he knew to be true about God and resolved to put his trust in God. David didn't know what the night might bring. He didn't know what the next day might bring. But he was confident that whatever might happen, God would see him through. Though the outcome was uncertain, David trusted that God had everything under control.

He concluded the psalm with this confident declaration: "In peace I will both lie down and sleep; for you alone, O LORD, make me dwell in safety" (v. 8).

The Bible teaches that God is sovereign. He is supreme—far above all rule and authority, power and dominion, and every title that can be given (Eph. 1:21). He reigns. He is in control. No matter what happens in our political, economic, or social structures. No matter what happens with our finances, our health, or our relationships. No matter what kind of havoc and destruction may come our way. We can be certain that heaven rules and that God is still in control.

We can rest confident, knowing "that neither death nor life, nor angels nor rulers, nor things present nor things to come, nor powers, nor height nor depth, nor any other created thing will be able to separate us from the love of God that is in Christ Jesus our Lord" (Rom. 8:38–39 csb).

When you fear God, you can confidently smile at the future. Not because you know what's going to happen but because you know that God is in control and he will be with you every step of the way.

THE RIGHT QUESTION

We started out by considering the question posed by Facebook's chief operating officer, Sheryl Sandberg: *What would you do if you weren't afraid?*

For some women, the answer may seem clear.

> Sue feels insecure about her appearance. She's always hated the shape of her nose.
>
> Melanie is anxious about her upcoming reunion. She doesn't want to face the embarrassment of showing up alone.
>
> Carrie is worried about the year-end meeting. She's afraid she'll be blamed for her team's poor performance.

Kelly wants to start her own business but is afraid to leave the security of her current job.

Melinda doesn't like the way her boyfriend talks to her sometimes, but she is afraid to say anything about it.

These women lack confidence. Some would say they just need to put on their big-girl pants and crush the fear that is standing in the way of their professional success and personal fulfillment.

What about women who are facing more substantive problems?

Becky fears that the lump in her breast is cancer.

Cindy's husband just died of a brain aneurysm. She's scared of raising their two kids alone.

Jessica's husband divorced her after thirty-six years of marriage. She struggles with arthritis and has no idea how she will manage. Instead of starting a retirement in Florida, she's starting a career at Walmart.

Odette fears for her son, who is a cocaine addict. Every time the phone rings, she dreads that she'll hear the news that he has overdosed and died.

Should we also tell these women to put on their big-girl pants and crush their fears? Should we challenge them with Sandberg's question, *What would you do if you weren't afraid?*

I think not.

Asking that question to a woman in crisis would be presumptuous. It would come across as glib and insensitive. It would trivialize the depth of her pain. These women are afraid. And for good reason. If we were in their shoes, we'd feel the same way.

You can relate. You've been there. And if you haven't, at some point you will be.

Implicit in Sandberg's question is the idea that it is possible to get rid of fear. She suggests that if we only had enough confidence, we wouldn't feel afraid.

But is getting rid of fear a realistic goal?

I don't think so.

Fear is in our wiring.

God created us to feel fear.

He created our brains with a fear system that involves four different circuits. Our alarm and association circuits are instinctive. Our evaluation and executive circuits are our volitional response to the automatic fear trigger. If our goal is to stop feeling afraid, we are kicking against the pricks. It won't happen.

We are creatures of fear.

And there's nothing we can do to change that.

Sin made fear run amok. When humanity fell, the emotion that God created for our good became a powerful tool of the Enemy. Ever since that fateful day, Satan has relentlessly used fear as a weapon against us. Therefore, while we live on this planet, we have about as much chance of getting rid of fear as we do of getting rid of evil. We fight the fight, to be sure. But until we see Jesus, the fight will not end.

All of us feel fear.

Feelings of fear can be sudden and intense or persistent and dull. They can range in intensity from anxiety, stress, and worry to panic, terror, and despair. Fear is something that crops up in our hearts virtually every day.

Eradicating fear is impossible.

Therefore, I think that the question *What would you do if you weren't afraid?* is entirely the wrong question. A better question is this: *What will you do when you feel afraid?*

FEAR IS AN INVITATION

What will you do when you feel afraid? Fear is an invitation. When fear comes knocking at your door (as it inevitably will), Satan wants you to respond the wrong way. God invites you to respond the right way.

You may view fear as a threat, but fear actually presents you with an incredible opportunity. From God's perspective, fear is

- an invitation to trust him,
- an invitation to examine our hearts,
- an invitation to send our roots deep,
- an invitation to experience a more wondrous fear, and
- an invitation to rest, gaze, and be awed.

To begin, fear is an invitation to trust the Lord. David said, "When I am afraid, I put my trust in you" (Ps. 56:3). Did you notice that David said *when* I am afraid and not *if* I am afraid? David anticipated that he would feel afraid.

Fear is to be expected.

Life is scary.

There are times when you will feel afraid.

David faced many stressful situations over the course of his lifetime. He had to flee for his life and stay on the run for years when King Saul went on a murderous tirade. The pressure didn't end when David became king. In fact, it intensified. Naysayers slandered him, crowds mocked him, friends betrayed him, family rejected him. Then there was that crisis with his son, Absalom. David faced political plots, assassination attempts, uprisings, and wars. What's more, he had to deal with the shame, self-reproach, and pain of making some extremely bad choices.

The psalms are replete with David's cries to God for help. They are also filled with declarations of David's resolve to put his trust in God and not in other things. Often, he cried out, "Deliver me, my God, from the power of the wicked, from the grasp of the unjust and oppressive. For you are my hope, Lord GOD, my confidence from my youth" (Ps. 71:4–5 CSB).

David made a habit of placing his trust in God. With God as his confidence, he was able to face even the most difficult circumstance with a peaceful, settled spirit.

What will you do when you feel afraid?

When fear comes knocking on your door, Satan wants you to trust his solutions. But God invites you to trust in him and lean on him. "Trust in the LORD with all your heart, and do not lean on your own understanding. In all your ways acknowledge him, and he will make straight your paths" (Prov. 3:5–6).

Second, fear is an invitation to examine our hearts. During the storm, Jesus asked the disciples, "Why are you so afraid?" (Mark 4:40).

Duh. Why do you think, Jesus? Isn't the answer obvious?

But it was a serious question and not a rhetorical one. Had they examined their hearts, they would have seen that at the root, the reason for their fear was not the storm but their lack of trust in God. The fear they felt was merely a symptom of a deeper problem.

Fear is like an indicator light on the dashboard of a car. When the indicator light starts flashing, it tells you that something is wrong and may require your attention.

Let's consider the common scenario of a woman feeling insecure about her appearance, for example. Perhaps she has a fresh scar on her forehead. Or a red, swollen, nasty zit. Or perhaps she hasn't lost those extra pounds of pregnancy weight. Instead of being excited to attend the party, she feels nervous—fearful—about people noticing or staring at what she views as a physical deficiency.

This feeling of fear is like a warning light on her emotional dashboard. It can indicate that she is putting her confidence in the wrong place. The fearful feeling can reveal to her that she is leaning on the fragile web of personal appearance, or on the affirmation of people, instead of relying on God.

Fear is a good indicator of where we are placing our trust. When we feel fear, it is an opportunity to examine whether we are trusting God more than we trust other things. Our hearts are desperately deceitful. We can be fooled to think we're trusting God. Only when our earthly security net is threatened, and the fear in our heart rises, are we able to discern where we are really placing our trust.

David prayed, "Search me, O God, and know my heart! Try me and know my thoughts! And see if there be any grievous way in me, and lead me in the way everlasting!" (Ps. 139:23–24). That's a great prayer to pray whenever fear comes knocking at our door.

Third, fear is an invitation to send our roots down deeper into God's living Word and living water. Fear reminds us that we desperately need God. We need his Word and his Spirit. Those are the things that give life to our spirits. Fear reminds us to send our roots deeper into the stream because things are heating up and our leaves are starting to droop.

Growing deeper roots is a constant need, of course. But when a crisis hits, we can discover that our roots are not nearly as deep as we thought they were. Or that they are not deep enough to handle the extreme, scorching temperatures that have suddenly hit. Fear is God's invitation to send your roots down into his waters. It's an invitation to dive deep into his Word and to walk by the power of his Spirit. As you do, he will provide you with what you need to remain green and bear fruit during even the most difficult drought (Jer. 17:5–8).

Fourth, fear is an invitation to experience a more wondrous fear. The fear of the Lord is the fear that conquers all fears. Reverent fear calms apprehensive fear. Whenever we feel apprehensive, that's God's invitation to draw near in awe, obedience, devotion, worship, and trust. David often begged God, "Give me an undivided mind to fear your name" (Ps. 86:11 CSB).

Before David became king, he and six hundred men took refuge from Saul in the land of the Philistines. Achish, king of Gath, gave them the town of Ziklag in exchange for military services (1 Sam. 27:2–6). Once, when David and his men were away on a military campaign, the Amalekites staged a raid on Ziklag, destroyed the city, and carried away all the inhabitants' wives and children. To make matters worse, David's men blamed him. "And David was greatly distressed, for the people spoke of stoning him, because all the people were bitter in soul, each for his sons and daughters" (30:6).

The situation was bleak indeed. How did David respond? The verse concludes, "But David strengthened himself in the LORD his God" (v. 6).

How did he strengthen himself?

He worshiped.

He let the fear of God wash over all his other fears.

I hope that this book has convinced you that not all fear is bad. Apprehensive fear is your enemy. But reverent fear is your friend. And the only way you will defeat the former is by embracing the latter. Reverent fear is the fear that calms all lesser fears.

Finally, fear is an invitation to rest, gaze, and be awed. When we feel anxious, we want to do something to resolve the situation. God wants us to stop feverishly trying to come up with our own solution. He invites us to stop striving. To rest. And to patiently wait on him.

When the Israelites were frightened by a political threat and tried, in their own strength, to outrun the problem, God challenged and rebuked them with these words:

> For the LORD GOD, the Holy One of Israel, has said:
> "You will be delivered by returning and resting;
> your strength will lie in quiet confidence.
> But you are not willing."
> You say, "No!
> We will escape on horses"—
> therefore you will escape!—
> and, "We will ride on fast horses"—
> but those who pursue you will be faster. . . .
> Therefore the LORD is waiting to show you mercy,
> and is rising up to show you compassion . . .
> All who wait patiently for him are happy. (Isa. 30:15–16, 18 CSB)

What does it mean to wait for the Lord? It doesn't mean frenetically trying to come up with our own solution. It doesn't mean tapping our foot impatiently waiting for God's answer. Waiting on the Lord means that we:

Stop.

Pause.

Rest.

And gaze at God in awe and wonder.

David longed to do this more than anything. He said, "I have asked one thing from the LORD; it is what I desire: to dwell in the house of the LORD all the days of my life, gazing on the beauty of the LORD and seeking him in his temple" (Ps. 27:4 CSB).

Remember the analogy of the diamond? When we wait, we let the light stream in. We, the creatures, kneel before our Creator and allow ourselves to be overwhelmed and awestruck by his indescribable power and beauty.

And we are undone.

Mysterium tremendum et fascinans.

Waiting on God puts everything in perspective. When we wait on God, lesser fears kneel to the Great Fear and lesser confidences kneel to the Great Confidence. Waiting on God helps us to see him and the world aright.

As we wait, something incredible happens.

His strength infuses us with supernatural strength and confidence.

Scripture promises that "they who wait for the LORD shall renew their strength; they shall mount up with wings like eagles; they shall run and not be weary; they shall walk and not faint" (Isa. 40:31). It indicates that "the fear of the LORD leads to life," and those who embrace this great fear rest content, untouched by trouble (Prov. 19:23).

Your fears, anxieties, and worries are an invitation to rest, gaze, and be awed by the God to whom belongs all glory, majesty, power, and authority before all time, now and forever. And to draw strong confidence from him.

REMARKABLE GRIT

As I write this final section, I reflect on what has been an extremely somber week. Tuesday was the one-year anniversary of the car accident that claimed my girlfriend Nanette's son, daughter-in-law, and two grandchildren. They were missionaries at an orphanage in Bulembu, Eswatini. The whole family was wiped out in one fell swoop. It was a horrific tragedy.

Nanette texted me and other friends on the anniversary of their death. She said:

> The earthly loss of Brendan, Melissa, Evelyn, and Colton has brought me to the brink of despair. At times, not knowing if I'd ever make it back. Hope is hard. Faith is a thread. But they are in the arms of the One they loved and served so faithfully. I live with the hope of eternity with Jesus and with my precious and beloved family. Your prayers have protected me from the one who would want to see me walk away. I WILL NOT! May my very broken hallelujah continue to give God all the glory.

Just after I received Nanette's message, I received the news that Nick Challies, the twenty-year-old son of other friends, Tim and Aileen Challies, had suddenly and unexpectedly dropped dead.

My heart felt so heavy . . . One-year-old grief and fresh grief all on the same day.

The day after the tragedy, Tim wrote:

> Yesterday Aileen and I cried and cried until we could cry no more, until there were no tears left to cry. Then, later in the evening, we looked each other in the eye and said, "We can do this." We don't want to do this, but we *can* do this—this sorrow, this grief, this devastation—because we know we don't have to do it in our own strength. We can do it like Christians, like a son and daughter of the Father who knows what it is to lose a Son. . . .

We know there will be grueling days and sleepless nights ahead. But for now, even though our minds are bewildered, and our hearts are broken, our hope is fixed and our faith is holding. Our son is home.[8]

I watched in sadness and wonder as Aileen stood with quiet confidence to speak at the memorial service to pay tribute to Nick and challenge listeners to make their lives matter.

Nanette and Aileen are my heroes. So is Melissa's mom, Michele. These women have tremendous grit. I'm sure they'd dispute this accolade, but it is true.

The reason I say they have grit is not because they are exceptionally gifted superwomen with impressive lists of accomplishments. They would say they are ordinary, just like you and me. It's not because they always feel strong and never feel afraid. When grief overwhelms them, they feel oh so vulnerable and weak.

So why do I say they have tremendous grit?

Because they are determined to put their confidence in God.

Even when it's hard.

Because of Christ, they say, we can do this. When Satan tempts them to walk away, they say, "I will *not!*" They do not *want* to walk these difficult paths, but they are confident that because the Lord walks with them, they *can* walk forward.

Their roots run deep.

In the midst of deep pain and anguish, their hope is fixed and their faith is holding. "The root of the righteous will never be moved" (Prov. 12:3). Yes, the drought is severe. But faith has not died. Though blistered by heat and withered, their leaves remain green.

I suspect that you picked up this book because you wanted to become a more confident woman. I hope I have challenged you to think about confidence in a different way. Strong confidence is not found in a strong feeling but in a strong Savior.

Some of you have had your world shaken by tragedy and loss, as my friends Nanette, Michele, and Aileen have. Others are just facing the usual assaults against confidence that go along with living in a fallen world. Like the fear of failure or embarrassment or fear of the future.

Whether your confidence battle is big or small, you can be assured that your confidence will grow strong and tall as the date palm or cedar when you grow in the fear of the Lord.

Women today are plagued with fears, insecurities, and anxieties. Popular wisdom tells us that the answer to this problem is to believe in ourselves more. But the Bible provides a different solution. It teaches that the way to combat fear is with more fear—fear of a different kind. A godly, reverent fear is what will transform us into bold, courageous, confident women.

Relying on God transforms your can't-do into a can-do. You can do all things through him who gives you strength (Phil. 4:13)!

As your fear of God increases, your fear of circumstances decreases. The fear of God changes you from

scared to secure,
    rattled to relaxed,
        panicked to peaceful,
          agitated to awed,
            bashful to bold,
              frightened to faith-filled,
                cowardly to confident,
                  and daunted to daring!

Becoming a reverent, God-fearing woman will alleviate your fears, reduce your anxieties, and infuse you with courage.

As the wise sage said, "In the fear of the Lord one has strong confidence" (Prov. 14:26).

The *right* kind of confidence!

NOTES

CHAPTER 1: A BLUEPRINT FOR CONFIDENCE

1. Sheryl Sandberg, *Lean In: Women, Work, and the Will to Lead* (New York: Alfred A. Knopf, 2013), 26.
2. Sheryl Sandberg, "Why We Have Too Few Women Leaders," TED Talk (Washington, DC, International Trade Center: TEDWomen 2010), video shared by TED Ideas Worth Spreading, December 2010, https://www.ted.com/talks/sheryl_sandberg_why_we_have_too_few_women_leaders.
3. Sandberg, *Lean In*, 8.
4. Sandberg, 24.
5. Judith Newman, " 'Lean In': Five Years Later," *New York Times*, March 16, 2018, https://www.nytimes.com/2018/03/16/business/lean-in-five-years-later.html.
6. "Our Mission," About, Lean In, https://leanin.org/about.
7. Laura Entis, "Sheryl Sandberg's Advice to Grads: Banish Self-Doubt, Dream Bigger and Lean In, Always," *Entrepreneur*, May 22, 2014, https://www.entrepreneur.com/article/234098.
8. Katty Kay and Claire Shipman, *The Confidence Code* (Nashville, TN: Harper Business, 2014), xii–xiii.
9. Kay and Shipman, xiii.
10. Maya Allen, "This Dove Report Reveals Shocking Results About Women's Body Confidence," *Cosmopolitan*, June 23, 2016, https://www.cosmopolitan.com/style-beauty/beauty/news/a60373/womens-body-confidence-declining/.

11. Claire Shipman, Katty Kay, and Jillellyn Riley, "How Puberty Kills Girls' Confidence," *The Atlantic*, September 20, 2018, https://www .theatlantic.com/family/archive/2018/09/puberty-girls-confidence /563804/.

12. Kay and Shipman, *The Confidence Code*, 21.

13. Dove, "New Dove Research Finds Beauty Pressures Up, and Women and Girls Calling for Change," PR Newswire, June 21, 2016, https:// www.prnewswire.com/news-releases/new-dove-research-finds -beauty-pressures-up-and-women-and-girls-calling-for-change -583743391.html.

14. Barbara Markway and Celia Ampel, *The Self Confidence Workbook: A Guide to Overcoming Self-Doubt and Improving Self-Esteem* (Emeryville, CA: Althea Press, 2018), x.

15. Kay and Shipman, *The Confidence Code*, xi.

16. "Self-Confidence and Self-Compassion with Sheryl Sandberg & Adam Grant," Option B, https://optionb.org/build-resilience /lessons/self-confidence-self-compassion.

17. Tony Robbins, "11 Tips for Being Confident from Within," Tony Robbins (website), https://www.tonyrobbins.com/building -confidence/how-to-be-confident/.

18. Kay and Shipman, *The Confidence Code*, 28.

19. Kay and Shipman, 50.

20. Thesaurus.com, s.v. "confidence," https://www.thesaurus.com /browse/confidence.

21. Thesaurus.com, s.v. "diffidence," https://www.thesaurus.com /browse/diffidence.

22. The Free Dictionary, s.v. "confidence," https://www.thefreedictionary .com/confidence.

23. Julie Andrews, vocalist, "I Have Confidence," by Richard Rodgers, Spotify, track 4 on *The Sound of Music*, 50th anniversary ed., RCA Victor, 1965; Legacy, 2015.

24. Charles Dickens, *A Tale of Two Cities* (1906; repr., London: J. M. Dent & Sons, 1914), 5, https://www.google.com/books/edition /A_Tale_of_Two_Cities/KBVXAAAAYAAJ?hl=en&gbpv=0.

CHAPTER 2: FEAR IS YOUR FRENEMY

1. Michel de Montaigne, *Essays of Montaigne*, trans. Charles Cotton, ed. William Carew Hazlitt, vol. 1 (London: Reeves and Turner, 1877), 69, https://www.google.com/books/edition/The_Essays _of_Montaigne/BnZAAAAAYAAJ?hl.
2. Dictionary.com, s.v. "fear (n.)," https://www.dictionary.com/browse /fear.
3. Power Thesaurus, s.v. "fear," https://www.powerthesaurus.org/fear /synonyms.
4. "Plutchik's Wheel of Emotions: Exploring the Emotion Wheel," Six Seconds (website), November 8, 2020, https://www.6seconds.org /2020/08/11/plutchik-wheel-emotions/.
5. ABC News, "Convicted Con Artist Reveals How He Scammed Others," uploaded November 21, 2014, YouTube video, 2:56, https://youtu.be /x3ggMKSbhOs.
6. Punita Shah, "Overcome Your Fear: 5 Steps to Become More Confident," Discoveri, July 23, 2019, http://www.talentdiscoveri.com /resentarticle.php?id=68.

CHAPTER 3: HELLO, MY NAME IS FEAR

1. "Fear," Oh Baby! Names, https://ohbabynames.com/all-baby-names /fear/.
2. "Fear."
3. Lexico, s.v. "fear (UK English)," by Oxford University Press, 2020, https://www.lexico.com/definition/fear.
4. *Webster's Dictionary 1828 Online*, s.v. "fear (n.)," http://websters dictionary1828.com/Dictionary/fear.
5. John Bunyan, *The Fear of God* (1679; repr., London: The Religious Tract Society, 1839), 138.
6. Bunyan, 66–67.
7. John Piper, "To Live Upon God That Is Invisible: Suffering and Service in the Life of John Bunyan," Desiring God, February 2, 1999, https://www.desiringgod.org/messages/to-live-upon-god -that-is-invisible.

8. Piper, "To Live Upon God."

9. Bunyan, *The Fear of God*, 142.

10. Bunyan, 139.

11. "NY Garage $3-Bowl Sells for $2.2m at Auction," BBC News, March 20, 2013, https://www.bbc.com/news/world-us-canada-21857435.

12. ScareHouse (website homepage), https://www.scarehouse.com/.

13. Allegra Ringo, "Why Do Some Brains Enjoy Fear?," *The Atlantic*, October 31, 2013, https://www.theatlantic.com/health/archive/2013/10/why-do-some-brains-enjoy-fear/280938/.

14. Eduardo B. Andrade and Joel B. Cohen, "On the Consumption of Negative Feelings," *Journal of Consumer Research* 34, no. 3 (October 2007): 15, https://papers.ssrn.com/sol3/papers.cfm?abstract_id=892028.

15. Patrick Sweeney, "Fear Is Fuel Will Teach You Courage," Fear Is Fuel (website), https://fearisfuel.com/the-book/.

16. Fearing your husband, in the context of Ephesians 5:33, simply means respecting him. It does not mean that you should be frightened of him. If you are fearful of being harmed, please contact a women's shelter. In the case of abuse, please call the police.

CHAPTER 4: THE FEAR FACTOR

1. G. Brad Lewis, *FireFall*, LavArt no. 22, G. Brad Lewis Photography, https://volcanoman.com/#/gallery/lavart/22-firefall/.

2. Rudolf Otto, *The Idea of the Holy: An Inquiry into the Non-rational Factor in the Idea of the Divine and Its Relation to the Rational*, trans. John W. Harvey, 2nd ed. (1950; repr., London: Oxford University Press, 1958), 10.

3. Otto, 15.

4. C. S. Lewis, *The Lion, the Witch and the Wardrobe* (New York: HarperCollins Publishers, 1950, renewed 1978), 146–47. Used with permission.

5. *Collins English Dictionary Online*, s.v. "awe," https://www.collinsdictionary.com/us/dictionary/english/awe.

6. *Webster's Dictionary 1828 Online*, s.v. "awful," http://www.webstersdictionary1828.com/Dictionary/awful.

7. Sandip Roy, "What Does Awe Mean: The Little-Known Power of Awe," The Happiness Blog, https://happyproject.in/awe-power/.

8. See 2 Timothy 3:1–5.

9. C. S. Lewis, *Mere Christianity* (Chicago: Musaicum Books, 2014), 63.

10. Andy Greene, "U2's Enormous Claw Stage to Become Permanent Installation," *Rolling Stone*, April 10, 2018, https://www.rollingstone.com/music/music-news/u2s-enormous-claw-stage-to-become-permanent-installation-629038/.

11. THR Staff, "U2's '360' Tour Will Gross $736.1 Million," *Hollywood Reporter*, July 30, 2011, https://www.hollywoodreporter.com/news/u2s-360-tour-will-gross-217411.

12. Bob Allen, "U2's Rose Bowl Show Breaks Attendance Record," *Billboard*, October 30, 2009, https://www.billboard.com/articles/news/266855/u2s-rose-bowl-show-breaks-attendance-record.

13. U2, "U2 - Where The Streets Have No Name (Rose Bowl 360 Tour)," posted January 23, 2013, YouTube video, https://www.youtube.com/watch?v=Eo8I3UQbW8s.

14. William Barclay, ed., *The Gospel of Matthew*, vol. 1, rev. ed., The New Daily Study Bible (Louisville, KY: Westminster John Knox Press, 2001), 445.

CHAPTER 5: FOUNDATION OF CONFIDENCE

1. "Kasia Urbaniak," Penguin Random House (website), https://www.penguinrandomhouse.com/authors/2198423/kasia-urbaniak.

2. Olivia Grant, "Female Confidence Gurus: Inside the Feminist Fad Taking New York By Storm," *Spectator*, February 18, 2020, https://spectator.us/topic/female-confidence-gurus-inside-feminist-fad/.

3. Kasia Urbaniak, "Under the Skin with Russell Brand: Attention and Domination," podcast interview with Russell Brand, transcript shared April 13, 2021, on Kasia Urbaniak (website), https://www.kasiaurbaniak.com/podcasts-on-air/under-the-skin-russell-brand-attention-and-domination.

4. Grant, "Female Confidence Gurus."

5. Kasia Urbaniak, "Influence 101: Liberating Your Desire and the

Power to Ask," Kasia Urbaniak (website), https://www.kasiaurbaniak
.com/power-influence-101-course.

6. Regena Thomashauer, Mama Gena's School of Womanly Arts
(website homepage), https://mamagenas.com/.

7. H. D. M. Spence and Joseph S. Exell, eds., *Pulpit Commentary*, vol. 1,
6th ed. (London: Kegan Paul, Trench, Trubner & Co, 1895), 87.

CHAPTER 6: CONFIDENCE BUILDING

1. Karen Abbott, "The Daredevil of Niagara Falls," *Smithsonian
Magazine*, October 18, 2011, https://www.smithsonianmag.com
/history/the-daredevil-of-niagara-falls-110492884/.

2. History.com Staff, "A Daredevil History of Niagara Falls," History,
updated October 23, 2019, https://www.history.com/news
/a-daredevil-history-of-niagara-falls.

3. Michael Greshko, "Galaxies, Explained," *National Geographic*,
April 17, 2019, https://www.nationalgeographic.com/science/space
/universe/galaxies/#close.

4. Jon Bloom, "You Obey the One You Fear," Desiring God, August 17,
2012, https://www.desiringgod.org/articles/you-obey-the-one-you-fear.

5. E. A. Hoffman, "Leaning on the Everlasting Arms," written in 1887,
hymn 133 in *The United Methodist Hymnal* (Nashville, TN: The
United Methodist Publishing House, 1989), Hymnary.org, https://
hymnary.org/text/what_a_fellowship_what_a_joy_divine.

CHAPTER 7: DEEPLY ROOTED CONFIDENCE

1. Shlomo Maital, "2,000-Year-Old Dates: Yummy!," *Jerusalem Post*,
October 15, 2020, https://www.jpost.com/jerusalem-report/2000
-year-old-dates-yummy-644620.

2. "Cedar Tree of Lebanon," Coniferous Forest, updated September 2,
2020, https://www.coniferousforest.com/cedar-tree-lebanon.htm.

3. Robert Jamieson, A. R. Fausset, and David Brown, *Commentary
Critical and Explanatory on the Whole Bible*, vol. 1 (Oak Harbor,
WA: Logos Research Systems, Inc., 1997), 663.

4. Jamieson, Fausset, and Brown, 663.

5. Answers (website), s.v. "How far do the roots of a cedar of Lebanon tree spread?", https://www.answers.com/Q/How_far_do_the_roots _of_a_cedar_of_Lebanon_tree_spread.
6. "Persecuted Church Statistics," The Esther Project, http://theesther project.com/statistics/.
7. "George Mueller, Orphanages Built by Prayer," Christianity.com, July 16, 2010, https://www.christianity.com/church/church-history /church-history-for-kids/george-mueller-orphanages-built-by -prayer-11634869.html.
8. Tim Challies, "My Son, My Dear Son, Has Gone to Be with the Lord," Challies (website), November 4, 2020, https://www.challies .com/articles/my-son-my-dear-son-has-gone-to-be-with-the-lord/.

ABOUT THE AUTHOR

Mary A. Kassian is an award-winning author and international speaker. She has published several books and Bible studies, including *Girls Gone Wise in a World Gone Wild*, *Conversation Peace*, and *The Right Kind of Strong*. She and her family reside in Canada.